GOD AND CONTEMPORARY MAN

GOD AND CONTEMPORARY MAN is one of the volumes in a new series, IMPACT BOOKS, designed to bring the modern reader the significant achievements of scholars, both Catholic and non-Catholic, in the fields of Scripture, Theology, Philosophy, Mathematics, History, and the Physical and Social Sciences. Among the titles in the series are:

What Is Philosophy? by Dietrich von Hildebrand
Modern Ethical Theories by James McGlynn, S.J., and Jules Toner, S.J.
The School Examined: An Essay on the Curriculum by Vincent Smith
Catholic Thought in Crisis by Rev. Peter Riga
Contraception and the Natural Law by Germain Grisez
Introducing the Old Testament by Frederick L. Moriarty, S.J.
This Good News: An Introduction to the Catholic Theology of the New Testament by Quentin Quesnell, S.J.
Maturing in Christ: St Paul's Program for Growth in Christ by George Montague, S.M.
Seven Books of Wisdom by Roland Murphy, O.Carm.

GOD
AND
CONTEMPORARY
MAN

REFLECTIONS OF
A CHRISTIAN PHILOSOPHER

ROBERT J. KREYCHE, Ph.D.

Foreword by
JOHN HOWARD GRIFFIN

THE BRUCE PUBLISHING COMPANY

MILWAUKEE

NIHIL OBSTAT:

    Rev. John E. Twomey, S.T.L., Ph.D.
    Censor librorum

IMPRIMATUR:

    ✝ William E. Cousins
    Archbishop of Milwaukee

    January 27, 1965

Library of Congress Catalog Card Number: 65–20264

© 1965 The Bruce Publishing Company
MADE IN THE UNITED STATES OF AMERICA

TO MY MOTHER

Who by the generosity of her Christian life
has spoken a wisdom greater than any to
be found between the covers of this book.

FOREWORD

Late one winter night in the 1950's, I placed a newly recorded tape on my machine and prepared to go to bed in the stone barn at my parents' farm near Mansfield, Texas, where I lived and worked. I had not yet recovered from the loss of sight suffered years earlier in a Pacific bombing, so I did most of my studying by tape. Above the sputter of a small gas stove, my reader's voice filled the narrow room. "*Logic*, by Robert Kraychy — his last name is spelled K-R-E-Y-C-H-E," she said.

I got from my bed many times that night to go make notes on the typewriter. It was my first contact with Robert Kreyche and it had a special tone. Although the book was purely scientific, its resonances in that room with its odors of stone and cigarette smoke and books and books and an underlying awareness of intense cold outside gave me an impression of solidity, strength, clarity; an impression similar to the fragrance of baking bread.

The following morning I wrote to Dr. Kreyche. I explained to him my growing concern over my lack of proper training in philosophy. My vocation as a writer was established with some initial success and I felt a keen responsibility to readers. Aside from fragmentary studies with the Dominicans in Paris and the Benedictines at Solesmes, I had no formal background in philosophy. I added that I had already begun to repair this lack by studying with the Discalced Carmelite Fathers of Dallas, mostly on tape, and that I was supplementing these studies with tapes from Gerald Vann, O.P., Jacques Maritain, and Etienne Gilson provided through the intervention of Father J. Stanley

Murphy, C.S.B., of Canada. I asked Dr. Kreyche if there were any way I could follow his course on tape as a special student.

Dr. Kreyche replied immediately, sent me copies of his examinations, and offered to help me in any way possible.

A short time later, Dr. Kreyche's work played an amusing role in a confrontation with a group of racists. I had begun to prepare some studies dealing with the problems of racism in our area. The head of a nearby White Citizens' Council telephoned to warn me to "keep my nose out of it."

"But you don't even know what I am writing," I told him. "I might be writing something favorable to you. Why should you threaten me before you find out what I am doing?"

"Do you mean you're for us?" the man asked.

"I'm looking for the truth," I said. "If you are in the truth, then nothing I say can offend you."

His voice warmed immediately and he offered to come to my workroom and "explain" things to me.

While waiting for his arrival, I put on the Kreyche tape and made an exact typewritten transcription of the chapter on traditional fallacies of logic.

The White Citizens' Council man brought a group of his friends with him. They entered my workroom and greeted me with overwhelming cordiality. For a half hour they enlightened me about racism as a patriotic and Christian virtue — nay, a duty.

When I began to question their viewpoint, they became suspicious and asked to know what kind of "stuff" I wrote.

"I write this kind of thing," I said, taking down the copy of traditional fallacies of logic and handing it to the leader.

He read aloud: "*Argumentum ad bacculum . . .*" hesitated, and added reproachfully, "Hell, it's not even in English."

"It turns into English with the next sentence," I said.

"An Appeal to Violence," he read, "where one seeks by force or violence, or threats of force or violence to win an argument that could not be won on its intrinsic merits." He continued down the list, skipping the Latin terms, reading in a grave and halting voice that somehow touched me. After he had rumbled through definitions of question-begging epithets, fallacies of the special case, and *ad hominem* argumentation, he interrupted himself. "Damn it, that's not fair," he shouted.

"What's not fair?" I asked.

"Accusing us of doing all those things. . . . "

One of his companions muttered: "We might as well go. We're wasting our time with the s.o.b. He's hopeless."

"But I haven't accused you of anything," I protested. "If you want to know the truth, I didn't even write that. It was written by a scholar who doesn't know you exist. But the shoe obviously fits, doesn't it? All of your rationalizations and racist arguments are identifiable fallacies of logic. You recognized all of these as applying to you and thought I was describing you. . . ."

The hierarchy of the White Citizens' Council stormed out in fury. I wrote of this incident to Dr. Kreyche, and since that time we have exchanged books and articles whenever either of us has published. In our exchanges, both personal and by correspondence, we have speculated about the broader applications of philosophy and theology, the deghettoizing of these disciplines. We were concerned with the formidable need to bring the lights of philosophy (in the sense of its being the Mother Science) and theology (in the sense of its dealing with concepts of the nature and destiny of man) to bear on the vast discovery of natural truths. Involved in all of this were difficulties of structure and scientific method — both necessary to ordered comprehension, but both too often tending to form virtual prisons from which truth could not escape to inform the activities of man, and into which new discoveries of truth could not always enter for fear they might endanger the structure. Too often one clung to the staleness out of fear that something was risked if the fresh air of new concepts

were allowed in. What does philosophy, after all, have to do
with man's daily existence? — with his shavings and his cook-
ing and his loving and suffering and bringing children to
light? At the practical level, the two were hardly on speaking
terms.

Who could read philosophy and theology except the
philosophers and theologians? In connection with this, Dr.
Kreyche and I speculated about the possible vocation of
the creative writer to take at least the major first principles of
philosophy and theology and transform them into art works
— drama, novel — so that their essences could be absorbed
as lived experience. The secret would be to take these only
as a springboard, not to tailor the work to fit the thesis, else
the work itself would be falsified. I set out on a massive
project of novels. Dr. Kreyche approached the same problems
within his own discipline — to open doors, to create an aura
of hospitality to ideas, to synthesize.

Working far more crudely, but still within a rigid structure, I wrote two novels. However, the first real experiment
came with a work of nonfiction, *Black Like Me*. This entire
experiment was conceived after I had studied at length
Jacques Maritain's analyses of racism, the fallacies involved,
and the remedies necessary to heal these profound wounds.
It was, if one can say such a thing, the gift of one's actions
to a superior truth revealed by Maritain rather than to an
inferior one at which I might have arrived myself. It was
simply Dr. Maritain's analysis made flesh.

Later I was to have close contact with the remarkable
Nobel Prize winner, Father Dominique Pire, O.P. This noted
Belgian theologian remarked to me: "For years I was a professor of theology and then one day I decided to stop teaching it and to begin to act it." His actions were truly spectacu-
lar, a sort of "theology fully realized," as the French say.

All of my own subsequent actions and writings, particularly on the subject of racism, are rooted in the soil of those
principles of philosophy as a mother science that I learned

from Dr. Kreyche and my other mentors. The results have
none of the appearance of science, I realize, but they grow
from that formation and without it I cannot imagine their
ever having grown at all. I recall Casal's constantly repeated
advice to his students: "Fantasy with order. Freedom with
order." I recall, too, the cellist's remark: "The first thing I
do on arising each morning is to play Bach — to cleanse the
atmosphere." Something of that "cleansing of the atmosphere" occurs in the great welter of natural truths when
one can welcome and order them into harmony.

This book, for which I have a special and personal affec-
tion, deals with these things. As Dr. Kreyche says, he is
handling a variety of ideas — tossing them at the reader in
the hope of creating a response. He attempts to open the
doors of the old prisons, not to discard or nullify what is old,
but to allow the eternal in it to come out and confront the
contemporary in a tempering fusion that can only benefit
both, and quite especially man. When one first opens the
door one glances a dazzling confusion, but a fascinating one.
It will take time and many minds to order this into harmony.
For the moment, the fact that doors are being opened — or
to be more exact, that men are *not afraid* to open them —
is the excitement of a book like this.

JOHN HOWARD GRIFFIN

PREFACE

This book is written for postmodern man. It is not a book of nostrums, "how-to" remedies, or easy cures for the problems of our day, but it does purport to deal on a very basic level with some of the problems that eat away at the very heart of man against the backdrop of the culture in which he lives. As to the format: most persons, whether as a matter of time, interest, or difficulty of concentration, find the reading of entire books in philosophy or theology a difficult, if not an impossible, task. Consequently, I have decided to write a brief volume of essays and reflections that are calculated to inspire and motivate the reader to the development of his own ideas.[1]

My purpose, then, is not to explore every possible avenue of approach to the topics treated, but — in the shortest possible way — to provide some fundamental insights. The book, therefore, will have achieved its purpose if the reader is satisfied that it has accomplished this purpose in his behalf. Further, whatever the format of this book lacks in the way of unity, it most certainly provides the reader with the opportunity of picking it up or dropping it at will and as the occasion demands.

No doubt the reader will be tempted to "quarrel" with various points the author tries to establish in this book. No harm, if "quarreling" in this instance means establishing honest points of disagreement. A controversial point here and there serves a far greater advantage than a method of procedure that only puts a reader to sleep. As for the question of originality, the reader must judge for himself. All that I personally claim is that the ideas I express are consciously at least my own, though I do not suffer the illusion that my own thinking is uninformed by the books that I myself have read. I lay claim therefore only to a limited originality and the same may be said for the use of terms. I have not con-

---

[1] This volume is only a modest effort at recasting some of the basic Christian themes that lie close to the experience of contemporary Christians in terms, it is hoped, that they can readily understand and penetrate.

sciously gone out of my way to invent new terms that would serve only to confuse the reader, and if a new term does crop up on occasion the reader may (it is hoped) assume that it serves some special need.

Within the course of this volume a fairly sizable number of quotations are used — not in order to draw up an anthology of authors — but only to provide fresh insights from different points of view. As regards subject matter, the work is admittedly a mixture of themes, some ancient and medieval, others new. By and large, however, the slant of the work is contemporary and it is written within the overall framework of the American milieu. At any rate, none of the themes are purely metaphysical, and the chief intent of the topics — somewhat disparately chosen — is to relate my own personal knowledge of philosophy, acquired over more than twenty years of teaching and study, to the sociocultural conditions of modern life. The present volume, therefore, is intended to give the reader some feeling, not only for the authenticity of the Christian tradition itself, but for the problems of contemporary man, especially in regard to the two key issues of God and human happiness.

As the reader may well judge for himself, this volume is neither a devotional treatise nor is it a purely philosophical or theological work. It is rather an attempt to portray realistically several of the combined insights of modern psychology, traditional philosophy, and theology. It is an attempt to help the reader to an understanding in depth of some of the key issues of our day. A central theme of this volume is the happiness of man, and it is in the light of this theme that the author hopes in his own way to provide a closer link between God and contemporary man.

In conclusion, I would like to thank Mr. William May of The Bruce Publishing Company for his encouragement in the production of the book.

Overland Park, Kansas　　　　　　　　Robert J. Kreyche
March, 1965

ACKNOWLEDGMENTS

We wish to thank the following for permission to reprint copyrighted material:

The Critic, for excerpts from "Culture and Morality" by Gerald Vann, O.P.;

Harcourt, Brace, and World, for citations from Joseph Krutch's *The Modern Temper*;

Harper & Row, Publishers, for citations from Erich Fromm's *The Art of Loving*, Pierre Teilhard de Chardin's *The Divine Milieu*, Pierre Teilhard de Chardin's *Letters from a Traveller*, Douglas V. Steere's *Work and Contemplation*, and Christopher Dawson's *The Historic Reality of Christian Culture*;

For permission to cite from *The Divine Milieu* we are also grateful to William Collins & Sons, and to Rosica Collins for citations from *Letters from a Traveller*;

Hawthorn Books, for excerpts from Regis Jolivet's *The God of Reason*;

Helicon, for passages from Jean Danielou's *The Scandal of Truth*;

Longmans, Green, and Company, for excerpts from Gerald Vann's *Awake in Heaven*;

Macmillan Company, for passages from Gustave Weigel's *The Modern God*;

Meridian Books, for citations from Jean Danielou's *God and the Ways of Knowing*;

The Newman Press, for passages from Arnold Rademacher's *Religion and Life*;

Charles Scribner's Sons, for excerpts from Jacques Maritain's *Reflections on America*;

The Society of Authors, for passages from Christopher Dawson's *The Crisis of Western Education*;

Sheed & Ward, Inc., for citations from Gerald Vann's *The Divine Pity*, Copyright 1946;

The World Publishing Company, for excerpts from Eugene McCarthy's *Frontiers in American Democracy*.

CONTENTS

PART TWO . . . *REFLECTIONS*

GOD AND CONTEMPORARY MAN

THE CHRISTIAN PHILOSOPHER AND THE CONTEMPORARY WORLD

To instruct the nation's youth is one of the finest ways of exerting one's influence as a philosopher — but it is not the only way. I am fully agreed, of course, that philosophy should play a vital role in the college classroom, but there is a great need as well for the creative development of philosophers themselves in order for them to achieve their own vocation, not merely as professors, but as philosophers.[1] I mention this point at the very outset if only to call attention to the fact that every philosopher — whether he is a Christian or not — should eventually become a philosopher for himself.

This statement can, of course, be easily misinterpreted to mean that no one should follow a master in philosophy, but that is *not* what I mean. As a matter of fact, unless one does follow a master over a long enough period of time he will in all probability end up in the "woods" of his own particular brand of relativism, positivism, or skepticism. I am not saying, therefore, that a man should not follow a master, but only this: at a certain point of one's philosophical development every philosopher should be prepared to express

---

[1] As a matter of fact, the confinement of philosophy to pure pedagogical routine can have a devastating effect on the development of our finest young philosophers, and it is one of the main points of this introductory essay to show the need, not for getting philosophy out of the classroom, but for getting it into the marketplace as well.

1

the truth as he himself sees it in the light of the needs of his times.[2]

All of this raises the question, of course, of what a Christian philosopher should be, and on this point I shall have to be brief.[3] In the first place I am in complete agreement with Etienne Gilson who has repeatedly stated that a Christian philosopher is something more than one who merely happens to be a Christian. He is or should be one whose philosophy is closely integrated with his Faith — even though the methods of his philosophy taken as such are a distinct source of knowledge from that which he knows by Faith. How all of this comes about is a difficult matter to resolve, but it should be stated quite categorically that no Christian philosopher worthy of the name should be a modern-day Averroist. This means that a Christian philosopher should not attempt to separate into airtight compartments his philosophy from his Faith, or worse yet to give his philosophy a role of preference superior to what he otherwise knows by Faith.

Concerning the various reflections that appear in the course of this volume, I have no illusions that they are the result of a "pure" philosophy, and it is dubious in any case that a Christian philosopher should be *only* a philosopher, i.e., a

---

[2] In my own view there is a creative potential in the young Christian philosophers of this continent that has hardly been exploited or put to use except in matters of sheer pedagogical routine. The problem, then, is not a lack of talent, but of the consumption of talent in all but creative endeavors. What this country needs, in the language of Professor Donald Gallagher of Boston College, is at least some Christian philosophers who can address themselves to their times in the way that William James addressed himself to his times. The need here is to build up a whole new tradition of Christian philosophizing in this country.

[3] Christian philosophers *seem* to suffer a disadvantage peculiar to themselves as Christians: should they speak out on matters pertaining to Revealed Truth they may be accused of "mixing philosophy with religion." Should they relegate their philosophy to a compartment by itself, they become Cartesian rationalists. Either way they jump they will be subject to criticism. This dilemma, however, is not the forbidding thing it appears to be, for it is possible for a Christian philosopher to do his thinking on an integral basis as a man. He need not worry, in other words, about being a methodological purist. To interrelate and integrate is not to bemuddle and confuse.

philosopher and nothing more. For one thing, it is a noble tradition dating back all the way to the ancient Pythagoreans to regard philosophy itself as something more than "pure theory": philosophy was for these men, as it was for Socrates and Plato after them, a *way of life*. Not that philosophy even among the ancient Greeks was a substitute for religion, but it blended closely in spirit and objective with the goals of a truly moral and religious way of life. A *fortiori*, then, this much should be acknowledged: although Christian philosophy is not itself a way of life, it is nonetheless a kind of wisdom that points holistically to a way of life that is integrally Christian. The ideal Christian philosopher, both in his thinking and in his whole way of life, is one who blends harmoniously the elements both of natural and supernatural wisdom.

Be all of this as it may, the main purpose of this essay is not to dwell in the abstract on what an ideal Christian philosopher should be, but to point up the need for commitment, for a commitment that calls for a growing realization of the social role of the philosopher — which is precisely to bring his insights to bear, not only on the speculative, but on the practical order of things and human affairs. *What the philosopher must do is to make his wisdom relevant to the culture and society in which he lives*, to speak out in a forceful and meaningful way on such subjects as natural law, human rights, the common good, and the like. To do this the philosopher must not allow himself to become bogged down by a too straitlaced and rigid commitment to purely rationalistic techniques of study, investigation, and proof, nor should he imagine that he is behaving as a philosopher only when he is formally demonstrating propositions.[4]

---

[4] For an example, would anyone regard Socrates as being anything less than a philosopher for having done one thing mainly — which was to draw people out by asking them the right sort of questions? The truth of the matter is that philosophers as men of flesh and blood should play a variety of roles and perform a variety of functions according to their own peculiar talents and dispositions. Nor should they be hidebound by any one single

As a basic point, then, let it be said that the philosopher should serve as a critic, as one who, according to the etymology of the term, knows how to judge (*kritein*) the spirit of his times. And if this role be rightly ascribed to the philosopher, it should not for that reason become the exclusive province of sociologists, economists, or even for that matter of theologians. On this very last point be it said that *the challenges which Christianity faces today cannot tolerate any internecine battles between Christian philosophers and theologians who are engaged in hairsplitting jurisdictional disputes.* In my opinion, then, whether a man be a philosopher or theologian, if he has a message to communicate relevant to the problems of his times, let him communicate that message in an atmosphere of complete intellectual freedom.

Until now I have been trying to say in effect that today's Christian philosopher should be something more than a medievalist, and even if he be a specialist in medieval studies, he has some obligation to show how the wisdom of the medievals has a message of importance for contemporary man. Beyond this, however, it must be said that the philosopher is not by vocation, as is commonly supposed, a purveyor of the abstract, but quite the other way around. Although the wisdom of the philosopher is in a sense all-embracing, it must be existential to the bone. The philosopher by vocation must judge of reality as it is, and this includes social reality as well.

True enough, the role of the philosopher as a wise man is a role of comparative transcendence. Yet the philosopher should not be so far aloof from his times that he is not also intimately associated with the culture from which he derives. This does not mean, of course, that he should become a child of his times in the sense of absorbing all the worst qualities of the society in which he lives. What it does mean is that he must be sufficiently a part of his own culture to

---

method of philosophizing, as though the purely technical methods of philosophy were the only ones that counted.

sympathize with its problems, to evaluate it from an empirical point of view, to judge it properly, and to provide some of the right kind of remedies for its ills. The philosopher, in short, must be able to assess both the good qualities and bad of the times in which he lives. He must know how to direct, to give teleological orientation to the forces — both rational and irrational — of his own native culture and traditions.

True enough, for anyone to become a philosopher worthy of the name there must (in the language of Toynbee) be a movement of withdrawal — that is, of withdrawal from the spirit of the world for the sake of a living, dynamic contact with truth. Yet there must also be a movement of return. If wisdom, philosophical or otherwise, tends to become too esoteric, it may well die on the vine. Every man, and the philosopher is no exception, has an obligation to his fellow-man. The Christian philosopher in particular is bound by a certain duty of love — not merely love of truth in an abstract sense, but love of fellowman — to bring whatever light he can to the agonizing problems of the world in which he lives. Like a modern John the Baptist, the Christian philosopher should in his own humble way be able to point the way to the side of truth and wisdom even when the sound of his voice is like that of a lonely prophet who cries in a wilderness of irrationality, confusion, and disbelief.

At least one of the roles of the philosopher should be that of making an *impact* on the times in which he lives, on the mind of his contemporaries. Although the philosopher's wisdom be in a *large* sense a traditional wisdom, it is not a "conventional" wisdom in the ironic sense in which John Kenneth Galbraith in his book *The Affluent Society* uses that phrase. Like Socrates, the philosopher must make his contemporaries more fully aware of their faults, foibles, and follies. Through a sort of maieutic or intellectual midwifery he must lead them to a rediscovery of the most intimate truths concerning their own distinctively human nature and something as well about the nature of God.

In recent years many significant books have been written about the predicament of contemporary man. These books have been written by literateurs, economists, political scientists, sociologists, and the like, but seldom — on this continent at least — by philosophers. Due to the silence of philosophers the general public has almost forgotten the fact that philosophers do have a social role — which must (whenever it is challenged) be vindicated. Beyond the question of right, however, there is also the further problem of making one's message effective, and on this point may I suggest that traditional philosophers take their clue from the existentialists.[5] Until now their approach to such questions as the "end of man," "human freedom," "conscience," and the like has been too neat, too wooden, too exclusively pedagogical, too highly demonstrative (in a mechanical sense) to make any decisive impact on the times. They have become so preoccupied with absolute methods of proof and clarity that they lose sight of the more far-reaching practical importance of the very topics themselves.

The outlook of mind I have been criticizing (let me call it the purely academic outlook) tends to remove philosophers from the conflicts of contemporary life and tends also to insulate them in a fortress of their own. Yet, to tell the truth, if they are to make any impact on their culture, philosophers in general, and Christian philosophers in particular, must learn to utilize these very conflicts, anxieties, and absurdities as the starting point of their social criticism. In any

---

[5] Most Christian philosophers are pedagogues, whereas the existentialists are for the most part literary critics and dramatists who are committed to the task of dealing with life as they find it. I mention this because pedagogically the "method of absurdity" (as used by the existentialists) is a poor one, at least on the surface. The student in the classroom doesn't like to be "shaken up." He much rather prefers to "take his philosophy" in neat parcels, clear-cut outlines, and in textbooks which contain little more than an abstract statement of principles. This, however, is not the only method of approach, not even the only pedagogical one. The other method is to confuse a person, to "shake him up" in the way that Socrates "shook up" the sophists, and then to let them fight their own way out of the morass.

event, there should be no dualistic separation in the mind of the Christian philosopher between reason and revelation, philosophy and theology, knowledge and life.[6]

Allow me, then, to summarize some of the things I have been saying thus far: that there is a need in our society for the philosopher, the Christian philosopher in particular, to give that society a sense of direction which it sadly lacks; that there is a great deal of fakery in contemporary life, and it is part of the practical wisdom of the philosopher to expose this fakery wherever it exists, whether in education, politics, or art; that the role of the philosopher as social judge and critic should not be preempted by men who might otherwise be less competent to play such a role.

On this last point it is all too true that so far as the "public philosophy" is concerned philosophers have had little effect upon it, and what is regretful here is not the pursuit of speculative wisdom as such, but the failure to communicate it to others.[7] Nor should the philosopher beg off his social obligations on the grounds that they might only add to the confusion. Confusion enough there is, but this is all the more reason why philosophers — if they have a clear-sighted vision of the truth — should make themselves heard. Better in this case to make mistakes and correct them than not to say anything at all, as it is only through a living dialectic that the full force of the truth of things will be made known. Never, then, should the Christian philosopher present the image of a man who is always at the point of saying some-

---

[6] To imagine that the Christian philosopher should always confine himself to philosophy alone is to make an unreasonable demand — is to ask that he become a sort of schizophrenic, that he maintain a split within his very consciousness between what he feels as a Christian and what he otherwise knows as a philosopher. To make a supposition of this sort is to posit a sort of Kantian dualism between the philosopher's beliefs and his pure philosophical knowledge taken as such.

[7] Note too the remark of F. H. Heineman: "My thesis is that, with some notable exceptions, most contemporary artists and philosophers have become partially, if not totally, technicians and that we are all in danger of suffering the same fate." *Existentialism and the Modern Predicament* (New York: Harper and Bros., 1958), pp. 17–18.

thing, but of one who can never quite manage to get the words out of his mouth.

If all that we have said is true, it is wrong for the philosopher to relegate his task as social critic to technocrats and psychologizing theorists of all sorts. What is necessary, perhaps now more so than ever before, is for the philosopher to curb his instinct for withdrawal in order to commit himself to the problems of modern society. Not everyone need agree, of course, with Plato's idea of philosophers becoming kings. Yet if philosophers are not or should not themselves be kings, it might not be a bad idea at least that they be the counselors in the sense of playing some kind of role as intellectual leaders of the society in which they live.

My intention is simply to make some sort of beginning along the lines suggested in this chapter: my role, though in a widely different sense than John Locke's, is that of a sort of underlaborer, if you will, whose main concern is that other persons reading this book will take up with the challenge it offers.[8] For my part I shall be satisfied if I have done no more than quicken the reader's realization of the importance of some of the topics that I have touched upon in these various sections. According to the spirit of this first introductory chapter much of the work of this volume will fall into the general area of "criticism." Self-criticism, however, or any other kind is a wholesome form of catharsis if put to proper use. Though not an absolute guarantee of social progress, it may yet provide the first step along the way. The purpose of this volume is to take that first step.

*   *   *

See also Topic Sixteen, Nos. 8 and 9;
Topic Twenty, No. 1.

---

[8] What counts here is not merely a prurient interest in these topics in the line of a fad, but a serious desire on the part of the reader to think them through for himself. The ephemeral interest of the quasi-professional dilettante is deceptive: once you have captured his attention you can never be sure of retaining it to the point where it really counts. In all matters of human importance it is personal appropriation, follow-through, and perseverance that matters most.

PART ONE · · · · · *ESSAYS*

CHAPTER ONE

SOPHISTRY: OLD AND NEW

A course in history of philosophy is incomplete unless it embodies some understanding of the sophists, and I write of sophistry here to show its relevance to the times in which we live. The ancient sophists were a group of men who stood intermediate, so to speak, between the pre-Socratics[1] on the one hand, and Socrates, Plato, and Aristotle on the other. In his *History of Greek Philosophy*, Burnet has this to say of the sophists:

> The Sophists quite naturally taught people who could pay them, and these were generally the well born and well-to-do. To a large extent, then, what they taught was the art of succeeding in a democratic State when you do not yourself belong to the ruling democracy, and, in particular, the art of getting off when you are attacked in the courts of law. That is the questionable side of the Sophist's work, but it is hardly fair to make it a ground of accusation against the men themselves; it was the natural outcome of the political conditions of Athens at the time.[2]

To the credit of the sophists it must be said that they played a vital role in the transmission of Greek cultural tradition, and some of them, like Protagoras and Gorgias, were

---

[1] The main concern of the pre-Socratics, such as Anaximander and Anaximenes, was speculative and directed to the cosmos as such. By contrast, the sophists were practical-minded men who concerned themselves with the cosmos of human affairs.

[2] John Burnet, *Greek Philosophy* (London: Macmillan and Co., 1950), pp. 109–110.

great teachers as well. Plato, however, objected to the sophists
on the grounds that they taught wisdom for a fee, and the
basis of his objection was as follows: wisdom, in the sense
of practical wisdom or prudence, is a virtue that cannot be
taught, so that anyone who attempts to teach it for money
is doing so on false pretenses.

The teaching of wisdom for a fee is not, however, the
most objectionable feature of sophistry as we know it among
the Greeks. On a doctrinal level sophistry is bad philosophy — and perennially so — because of a basic relativism. As
Protagoras put it, man is the measure of all things — of those
that are that they are and those that are not that they are not.
From this point of view, there is or can be no such thing as
universal truth of the sort that man encounters in things
themselves or in his very own nature, since it is man himself
who makes the truth. This doctrine is in many respects the
ancient predecessor of the more modern pragmatism that
tends to identify the true and the good.

For purposes of this essay I want first to examine Plato's
definition of a sophist and, second, to show that sophistry
in its more pejorative meaning is not a thing of the past.
As for Plato's definition, the viewpoint he expresses is this:
the sophist is not (in the way that Socrates was) a truly
wise man. True enough, the sophist claims to know the
answers to many things, as did Hippias the Polymath, and
he is quite versatile in the art of rhetoric, but he is not
on that account a truly wise man. Here the reader may recall
that Socrates' quest for a wise man resulted in the dis-
closure by the Oracle of Delphi that he himself of all men
in Greece was the wisest and the best. Finding it hard to
believe this, he nonetheless made a sort of profession of
exposing the sham wisdom of the sophists only to find in
the end that whereas all of these men thought they knew
the answers to life's problems he was the only one among
them who knew that he did not know. Socrates' wisdom, in
other words, was that of a sort of learned ignorance, the

kind of wisdom that was fully aware of its own limitations.

All of this, then, brings us to Plato's definition of a sophist as being a person who, lacking wisdom, nonetheless displays its appearances. To enlarge on this somewhat, the sophist to Plato is one who through rhetorical devices can trap others into thinking him to be wise whereas in reality he is not. Further, he is one who through fallacious arguments can make a half-truth appear to be the whole truth; he is the sort of person whose central concern is not the objective truth of things but his own practical advantage.

This much for a definition of a sophist. The question now is whether it is altogether bad for a person to be a sophist, and I suppose a distinction or two is in order. Surely, if being a sophist means no more than simulating truth, then being a sophist is equivalent to being a liar — which, as all honest men will agree, is bad. There is another sense, however, in which I would wager that most men are sophists at heart, the sense in which all of us who have some measure of pluck will do our best to influence others to our own way of thinking through cajolery, rhetoric, or good-natured "kidding." Being a sophist in this sense is not unrelated to being "downright human," and none but a stoic would say that this is altogether reprehensible or bad.[3]

This granted, the conditions of modern society are still a standing witness to the fact that sophistry in its bad sense is as much alive today as ever it has been in the past. Take modern advertising for an example. It is quite generally known that the Madison Avenue techniques of selling a product are far less concerned with the intrinsic worth of the product itself than they are with the "projection of the right kind of image." In an excellent article entitled "The

---

[3] Is it not reasonable, after all, for a politician to present arguments for his party, arguments that will throw it in a favorable light, or for a salesman to play up the advantages of his product? Surely, where no absolute certainty can be had it is perfectly legitimate to point up the positive features of one's product whether it is a question of winning a vote or selling a washing machine. A society in which no competition prevails might easily tend to stagnate.

Image Revolution" one author makes it quite clear that a hidden revolution has been going on in American life roughly since the end of World War II. This revolution

> rests on the assumption that reality is something highly subjective . . . that man is shaped not so much by reason and ideas as by a visual-psychological field.[4]

The main point of this particular article, which comes to grips with the sophistry of image-projecting, is that the appeal to the prospective consumer is not in terms of what he gets, but rather of what he *thinks* or, better yet, of what he *imagines* he is getting. Thus automobiles are sold, not chiefly as a means of transportation but as a symbol of pleasure, power, or prestige. In a similar vein, modern advertisers often fabricate statements which, although seemingly innocuous, nonetheless achieve their intended effect. Take the following bit of cigarette advertising as a case in point: "No medical evidence or scientific research has established our brand to be inferior to any other product." This statement says very little, but coming at the time that it did — after the government issued its report on the medical dangers of cigarette smoking — it tended to diminish these fears in the mind of unreflecting persons who read and were influenced by this ad.

In the light of examples like this there is, accordingly, a need to exercise control over those segments of society, especially in the advertising world, that tend, as the saying goes, "to get out of hand." In fact, were it not for the efforts of government to protect an unwary public against inferior wares, the situation would be much worse than it is today. There is a point, after all, beyond which casuistry has its limits, and it is one of the functions of government to see to it that these limits be carefully guarded and stringently observed. Moreover, it is good for professional organizations to protect themselves against sophists within their own

─────────
[4] Neil P. Hurley, S.J., "The Image Revolution," *America*, Vol. 110, No. 4, Jan. 25, 1964, p. 137.

groups, and this can be done to some extent by the enforcement of their own codes of ethics.[5]

On this last point I want to suggest (though it takes no great philosophical acumen to do so) that the best guard against quacks and sophists is a public that is properly informed whether through newspapers and journals or any other means. The assumption here is that every society consists of two elements: those persons who in some way or another contribute to the common good, and those who do not, and by "those who do not" I mean those persons who positively militate against the common good by deceit, collusion, or any other means. It is persons of this sort against whom the public should be protected at all costs.

I have just suggested the need for a *well-informed* public. Beyond this the public — or at least a substantial segment of it — should be *well educated* besides. This means that people should not only be enlightened by *facts*, but they should also be taught the *principles* whereby they might judge the facts. Not *any* education will, of course, serve this purpose, but only one that is based on a solid ethical foundation, on the foundation of principles that accord with the universal nature of man himself and man's common good.

Here I would venture to say that the best kind of education is one that enables a person — over whatever period of time it takes to do so — to learn the all-important *art of discrimination*. It may appear strange that I should make discrimination out to be the very end of the educational process, especially in a society in which discrimination, especially of the racial sort, is the very thing we hope most to eliminate. But this latter is not obviously what I mean: what I do have in mind is the need for making the right kind

---

[5] Generally, it is recognized that there are hacks and quacks in the field of business and politics. But it should be equally known that there are quacks or near-quacks in the medical profession, in the educational world, in law, in entertainment, and so on. How to eliminate the quacks is a problem that will continue as long as man walks the face of the earth, but the point is that effective measures must always be taken to keep them in check.

of discrimination between what is merely meretricious and ephemeral and what is basically sound, between the true and the false. In one sense the best educated person is the one who has the "best taste," and this concept is not too far removed from the root meaning of wisdom, of *sapientia*, the *taste* for what is best, for what is noble, for what is sound.

For an example, sophistry in the field of art could be eliminated or minimized if people knew how to judge and *discriminate* between good and bad art; sophistry in business could be eliminated or minimized if, again, people became more acutely aware of the dangers of the "hidden persuaders," and so on in every other field. President Kennedy, quoting Scripture, once said in a public address that "where there is no vision the people will perish," and it is no small advantage for the people to get the kind of education that will rear, not a generation of fadists, dilettantes, eclectics, and neo-sophists, but a generation of people who have a taste for the common good.

In the light of what we have said it would follow, then, that the great need of civilization is to be purged of the overweening influence of sophistry. This means that a well-educated public must always be on its guard against pseudo intellectuals, pseudo revivalists, pseudo artists, pseudo political leaders, pseudo workmen, and the like. No society can ultimately survive in a situation in which everyone preys on the ignorance of his fellowman. The problem, then, is not to eliminate sophists, as this would be altogether impossible, but to develop the kind of taste, discrimination, and sense of criticism that will make it difficult for them to survive.

*　　*　　*

See also Topic Three, Nos. 1–4.

CHAPTER TWO

ON PLATO'S REPUBLIC:
EXCERPT FROM A STUDENT'S REPORT

A professor's penance is, so to speak, a built-in feature of his professional work, especially in the matter of correcting term papers and students' reports. Over the years I have searched deep in my subconscious for something new or different to say by way of personal comment and correction. Yet in spite of all this I usually come up with the following typical comments: "good," "very good," "excellent," "fine observation," "please give bibliographical reference," "use subheadings," and so on.

Even so, a glimmer of sunshine occasionally peers through the clouds, and such a glimmer came one day as I picked up a student's report on Plato. What interested me about this report was not so much its style (as the style was quite ordinary), nor its depth, but its sincerity and good sense: the student had enough good sense to apply something he had learned in Plato to his own personal life and times. At the very beginning the student expressed his hope of someday becoming a government worker. Not a very ambitious task, you might say, as there are millions of government workers, yet I would venture to say that if this student's ambitions are fulfilled in however modest a fashion, he will be quite different from these millions. Some of the reasons for this may be gathered from the balance of this essay.

The student in question chose to make his report on Books VIII and IX of Plato's *Republic*, which deal with the various forms of government such as tyranny, monarchy, oligarchy, and democracy. The point of interest, however, is not these various forms of government but the student's interest in Plato's discussion of democracy and the bearing that it has on modern life. As he expressed it:

> While scanning the dialogues, my interest was aroused by the conversation between Socrates and Plato's brothers (Glaucon and Adeimantes) in Book VIII. However, I was further amazed at the seemingly close parallel between a section of the discussion and the facts of modern living in the United States, and I decided that such an accurate account of society, given over 2000 years ago, merited more than just a cursory perusal.

The report continues with some few words as to the difference between just and unjust forms of government and then proceeds as follows:

> Having experienced life solely under the democratic form of government, I was particularly intrigued with Plato's discussion of democracy. To paraphrase some of the dialogue, the democratic man spends his time, labor, and money on unnecessary as well as necessary pleasures; he scorns advice, denying any difference between good and evil desires, saying that one is as good as another. *"He lives from day to day indulging the appetite of the hour; and sometimes he is lapped in drink and strains of the flute; then he becomes a water-drinker and tries to get thin."*[1] This passage completely overwhelms me! It should suffice to say that we have only to look about us to see the above accounts in reality.

Look about us indeed! Little could Plato surmise that a world of technology would someday provide antacid formulas for people who eat too much; that man would take up smoking and then invent new chemical formulas for its prevention; that he would someday invent a diet of sweets to please his palate only to fluoridate his water to prevent tooth decay. On a yet more serious vein, however, the report proceeds as follows:

> Such lucid descriptions should stimulate a moderate level of interest in anyone reading Plato. They raise man's thoughts

---

[1] Italics mine.

from his dream world into the cold, stark world of objective reality. They may aid the more educated in realizing and accepting the existence of an immutable natural law, and a moral code, whereby the shell of subjective idealism is broken, permitting the just man to emerge.

And "Who is the just man?" we may ask:

In Book IX, Plato reveals the qualities of the just man, from which we are able to discern the core, the rational fore-runner of Christian morality. The just man will cater to the soul, which is more honorable than the body, and will not yield to irrational pleasures which may upset the harmony of the soul. He will regulate his pursuit of riches, and will accept those honors which he deems likely to make him a better man.

Barring the hint of dualism in the contrast here between body and soul, it is true nonetheless to say that Plato has pinpointed a fundamental weakness of our times which is the failure "to cater to the needs of the soul." To give the soul, as it were, a chance to breathe, an opportunity to recollect itself in the midst of distractions, to see the manifold of our daily life in the light of a unifying principle that gives meaning and depth to our lives — this is one of the greatest needs of our times.

As an answer, then, to a professor's dream the report concludes as follows:

In summary, Books VIII and IX were a pleasant, stimulating introduction to Plato, since I am a newcomer to the dialogues. The method of discourse made the reading an interesting and lively experience, and thus further whetted my appetite for philosophical study. This brief venture into the mind of Socrates has stimulated some self-reflection on my part concerning my values, ideas, and opinions. In fact, the lucid descriptions and easy style of the Socratic dialogues should stir a moderate level of interest in most anyone who reads them. The exact effect may be left to speculation, but nevertheless, these dialogues are fresh food for thought.

*   *   *

See also Topic Two, Nos. 1–8.

CHAPTER THREE

PLEASURE AND ANTIPLEASURE: ARE CHRISTIANS NECESSARILY STOICS?

On return from Mass on a beautiful late fall morning I met a bachelor friend of mine who invited me to his house for what turned out to be a hearty breakfast of bacon and eggs. While discussing biology with my friend (he was a biology professor) I suddenly realized that it was time to get to my ten o'clock class in Greek philosophy. The class on this particular morning was devoted to the study of the Epicureans, and what follows is pretty much an account of what I had spoken of in my lecture, digressions and all.

What then of the Epicureans? Should I spend all sorts of time discussing with the class their outmoded physical theories? Hardly so, since the *forte* of the Epicureans was their doctrine relating to ethics and philosophy of life. Indeed, for Epicurus (341–270 B.C.) philosophy *is* a way of life: it is for him a practical activity intended by means of speech and reasoning to secure a *happy* life. As for the means of achieving happiness (and this long before the days of tranquilizers in their modern form) it was held that the good life is one which begins and ends in pleasure. *All human endeavor should be focused on the fulfillment of the pleasure principle.*

But here is where the problem begins, as "pleasure" to the

Epicureans is not to be taken indiscriminately, but only from the standpoint of what leads to the overall enjoyment of life. What Epicurus recommends, in other words, is not the indiscriminate pursuit of sense pleasure for its own sake, but the subordination of it to the control of reason which exercises moderation in all things. Understood in this sense Epicureanism is a far cry from, let us say, an open invitation to a Bacchean banquet or to some form or another of debauchery. A man who so indulges in pleasure is not an Epicurean at all, but a fool.

At this point every Christian will admit, I trust, that Epicureanism as a philosophy of life is false or at the very least one-sided. Yet to be fair-minded about it one should also see the positive merit of this philosophy, namely, that pleasure is one of the basic goods of all human life. Historically, however, this has not been the case, as many Christians have more often been Stoics at heart than Epicureans. Among such Christians the trend has been in the direction, not of the enjoyment of life, but of a certain type of manichaeanism, jansenism, calvinism, and, on American shores, puritanism — all of which forms of rigorism tend to squelch the value of the pleasure principle in human life.

Christian asceticism, of course, is one thing, that is, as a means of securing moderation in all things, as a means of practicing the virtue of temperance. Yet the perverse influence of various philosophies alien to the true Christian spirit has actually led many Christians to think that in order *to be happy in the next life you have to be miserable on earth* — and nothing could be further from the truth. Briefly, let us examine the view of so many Christians that their own way of living must be based on a rejection of pleasure as a fundamental type of human good.

In such a view it is thought — consciously or otherwise — that to "give in" to feelings of enjoyment is, as it were, to succumb to some kind or another of temptation, as when one thoroughly relishes a good meal, a good dance, a good movie, and so on. "Moderation" for such persons means "no real enjoyment." Go along with other persons in the doing of these things, and let them have fun, but don't get too much of the spirit of fun yourself lest you become tainted with a sort of worldly spirit that will interfere with the attainment of your final end.

Particularly in regard to the use of sex in marriage does such an outlook engender a sort of split within man's psyche. On the one hand, it is known (as a matter of intellectual conviction) that marital intercourse is perfectly good and wholesome, and yet it is feared that the pleasure attached to this act is wrong. Such a view, I say, can lead to unhappy results, and in view of this it is important to know that the pleasure of sex in marriage, like all other pleasure, is a human good that accompanies the exercise of a human power as its natural reward. To reject this pleasure is to reject one of the reasons why two persons get married in the first place — that is, because they were physically attracted to each other, even though, let us hope, there was much more to it than that.

This point that pleasure really is one of the fundamental goods of life must be solidly established in the mind of every Christian if only for the negative purpose of avoiding what has become a preponderant factor in modern life, namely, neurotic guilt. The whole psychological setup of a person who feels that he is doing something wrong when he is doing something eminently right, that is, in the enjoyment of legitimate pleasure, can only lead to a guilt complex. One goes about feeling he has done wrong by "allowing" himself, i.e., tolerating a certain pleasure and goes on beating his breast in the confessional for no more than imaginary sins. He becomes progressively introspective and scrupulous and ends up wasting a lot of good time and energy over what in the objective order is "nothing at all," but what subjectively becomes a burden too heavy to bear. Needless to say, stoicism, rigorism of this sort is too hard to bear over a long enough period of time and in the end often leads a person to do something that is really wrong, as when one in order to escape his problems (real or imaginary) becomes an alcoholic.

The point of this entire discussion, then, is to show that pleasure is in no sense an evil except when one pursues pleasures that are wrong for the person involved or pursues the right ones as an end in themselves. Surely, God did not make man to live only for pleasure, and, oddly enough, if one does pursue pleasure as the only worthwhile thing in life he ends up with no real pleasure at all. Such a person has no deep sense of lasting satisfaction, no peace, no spiritual joy, and the very pleasures that he pursued with so much obsession and intensity ironically turn against him and take on the aspect of pain.

On the other hand, to reject all pleasure, to cast it out as a sort of evil, even from the highest motives, is to do violence to the psyche, to create a false split that will in due time cause disruption and loss not only of ordinary human enjoyment, but of spiritual peace. This is not to say, of course, that asceticism is wrong, but only this: *to become an ascetic from the wrong motives is a bad thing.* If a monk gives up many of the legitimate pleasures of life to pursue a higher calling, he does so, not to escape these pleasures as though they were evil, but to find joy in a yet higher mode of life which brings with it certain pleasures of its own that the undisciplined person will never learn to enjoy. Strangely enough, or not too strangely at all, although a saintly person allows himself only a few simple pleasures in life, he has a much keener enjoyment and appreciation of them than the profligate. The experience of a dissolute king in the presence of an unlimited supply of roast beef, mistresses, and wine is one of surfeit, nausea, and disgust — with himself and his environs — whereas contrariwise the experience of a simple monk, who cultivates a patch of strawberries, is one of contentment and peace.

As against the extremes, therefore, either of rejecting pleasure, especially for the wrong reasons, and of pursuing it as if nothing else mattered, the right attitude of mind is to enjoy the goods that one has and to be thankful for their enjoyment. A free Christian spirit is unfettered by any false sense of guilt; it is dominated further by a desire to bring pleasure to others. It is part of Christian charity, I would imagine, not only to provide for the necessities of our fellowman, but to provide as well for some superfluities that add to his pleasure and enjoyment. If this were not so, parents would be wasting their time, money, and energy in the purchase of attractive gifts for their children at Christmastime or other times of the year. Although no Christian should be an Epicurean at heart, neither is it his calling to play the role of a killjoy or of a quasi-professional stoic.

To anyone, therefore, whose past is tainted with stoicism I can only offer the following words of advice written to me by a friend who is one of the finest Christians I know:

> Recognize in the depth of your being that the body and the sense appetites cry for the sunlight of God's love as much as the rational being, that many superficial precepts of morality must be considered just that — and especially those that truncate the naturally functioning man; that one must come back out of the darkness liberated in a sense from contempt for any of those things which God created as good; and therefore deeply involved in nature and *without fear*; in fact, capable of loving many of these very things which have been the cause of fear and repression in one's past.

*   *   *

See also Topic One, Nos. 1–13.

CHAPTER FOUR

SELF-LOVE: TRUE AND FALSE

It is often thought that the essence of true humility is to "run oneself to the ground," and no idea could be more mistaken than this. Unhappily, the world is filled with persons whose greatest fault is a false estimation of themselves, with the kind of persons who are ready to put themselves on the block when there is no real need to do so. Indeed, self-love in the pejorative sense of the term is one of the most subtle of all human defects, and it masks itself most often in the very attempt to belittle oneself.[1] All too often the person who deprecates himself is merely using a device (consciously or otherwise) to evoke the sentiment of pity in someone else and on one's own behalf, and such a practice is a complete distortion of the virtue of humility. The point here is that if we really love ourselves we must truly forget ourselves, and not constantly be at pains to say how worthless we really are.

The purpose of this essay, however, is not to point out all

---

[1] St. Thomas has some remarkable thoughts on this subject: "Since the wicked do not know themselves aright, they do not love themselves aright, but love what they think themselves to be. But the good know themselves truly, and therefore truly love themselves . . . as to the inward man . . . and they take pleasure in entering into their own hearts. . . . On the other hand, the wicked have no wish to be preserved in the integrity of the inward man, nor do they desire spiritual goods for him, nor do they work for that end, nor do they take pleasure in their own company by entering into their own hearts." *Summa Theologiae II–II*, Q. 25, a. 7, as quoted by Reginald Garrigou-Lagrange in *The Three Ages of the Interior Life*, Vol. I, p. 42.

or most of the aberrant forms of self-love. That would be an impossible task since every moral fault (from the misuse of sex to the stealing of apples) is in some remote sense connected with a mistaken love of oneself. Rather I should like to focus on the meaning and necessity of true self-love to show something of its importance in relation to the love of our fellowman. My personal thoughts on this subject have been largely inspired by two philosopher friends of mine in Minnesota who as husband and wife have given a great deal of attention to the meaning of love. I quote from one of them as follows:

> In the relation of give-and-take, giving is a willingness to become possessed by another; it is a readiness to become an object for someone else. Such giving is a deeply regressive act of yielding one's subjectivity into the hands of an objectifying agent. The subject who is willing to become an object is not one who firmly and lovingly stands in the transcendental finality of his own existence. Willingness to become possessed is the deepest, and often the most subconscious form of self-negation; it is the hidden suicide that sometimes leads to suicide with the gun or knife.[2]

If I rightly interpret the passage above, what it fundamentally means is this: although all love consists in a giving of sorts, it does not consist in a *giving over* of oneself to another as a toy or an object to be handled at will by the one to whom the surrender is made. This implies further that the meaning of love in its true sense is founded on the notion of a *self* (with a finality of its own) that is *free*. True enough, all love involves an element of surrender, of risk, a giving of self to another. That act of surrender, however, to be meaningful in a deeply human sense must be *free*, and to be free it must be based on a prior understanding and love

---

[2] From "The Meaning of Friendship," delivered by Mary Rosera Joyce to the North Central Group of the American Catholic Philosophical Association, October 26, 1963. This paper has been published under the title "Strangers in Paradise," *Delta Epsilon Sigma*, Vol. IX, No. 4 (Dec., 1964), pp. 141–145.

of oneself (interpreted in the very best sense of the term).
The author of the quotation above continues as follows:

> A real act of giving is not possible for a subject who does
> not know what it means to stand firmly and lovingly in the
> finality of his own existence. By loving himself, not primarily
> for the sake of the lover . . . the human person frees his
> power for loving other beings for their own sake, as final
> ends in themselves. In this freedom, he transcends the psy-
> chological, subject-object zone of possessing and being pos-
> sessed; he enters the here-and-now transcendental world
> where the relation between subjects is a receiving kind of
> giving and a giving kind of receiving.[3]

The implication here, as I grasp it, is basically this: unless
a person in loving someone else has first a true love of himself, he has little or nothing to give. This love of self is based
on an estimation of one's true worth and a desire to communicate the goodness that one possesses — as his own — to
another. To make this idea as concrete as we possibly can,
consider the man who wants to marry a woman mainly, let
us say, to make her comfortable with the things that money
can buy. Although there is a love of sorts in a situation like
this, it is an imperfect love because the estimation of self
and the giving of self is too closely bound up with the sharing
of a purely external good. The love is imperfect because
the "medium of exchange" is imperfect and of a highly
impersonal nature. By contrast, take a young man of paltry
means who makes a proposal of marriage to a young lady
equally as poor as himself, but with the utmost conviction
that it is possible for him to make her happy. Such a love
has a far better chance of surviving because it is based, not
only on a faith in the person who is loved, but on a faith
in oneself in spite of the lack of financial security and other
external means. Love of this sort can, at times, prove to be
heroic, though, needless to say, the love that most persons
have of each other, though constant, is often far from heroic.

---

[3] Ibid.

Paradoxical as it may seem, a true and perfect love is based on a genuine knowledge and love of oneself, and from the standpoint of Christian philosophy this is the kind of love that God has of Himself. Though it be a scandal to some, God created the world because of the love which He has for *Himself*, and it would be impossible on metaphysical grounds to make any claim to the contrary. The will of God, in other words, could not have been determined from without as though it were dependent on something other than itself, and it is this very fact which makes Creation the *free* act that it is. God created *freely* because loving Himself necessarily, He wanted to share that love with the world that He creates. The source, in other words, of His divine creativity (taken here in an absolute sense) is nothing less than the knowledge and the love that God has of Himself. Thus:

> Because God loves His own Being so fully, He is infinitely free to create beings other than Himself. If God loved Himself less, He would be reluctant to create other beings. Evidence of God's great love for His own being is the multitude and variety of beings in the world. If I would love my own being more, I would become more ready, more free, to love others, to create in my consciousness an awareness of others as ends in themselves, that is, as subject, not only as means, as object, as things exteriorized in being possessed by me.[4]

To summarize all this we may say then that love of others is an overflow of the good that lies within ourselves. We consolidate that good when we communicate it to others whom we regard, not as means, but as ends. We do an injustice to ourselves and our Maker if we brutalize ourselves by beating down true love of self. Each man has a unique mission to perform that redounds to the good of others, but only because of and through the goodness that one already possesses and has appropriated as one's own. As the saying

---

[4] *Ibid.*

goes, *Nemo dat quod non habet* — "No one can give what he lacks."

One further point is worth noting. The higher the order of the good we possess the less we lose in the communication of that good to others. A professor does not make himself ignorant by communicating his knowledge to his students. Even so, *there is one sense in which it is a mistake to be all things to all men,* namely, the sense in which we diffuse ourselves to the point of losing our identity as authentic selves. The good that we do lies precisely in conferring the mark of our own identity, of our own personality and character on our work and on our relations with other persons. Thus the philosopher (to benefit others as a philosopher) must remain true to his own vocation, and each person must remain true to the more fundamental vocation that *is himself.* The secret of happiness does not lie in being something other than we are, in putting on some kind of mask or playing a role, but in being our own true and authentic selves. It may take a lifetime to discover the self that we really are, and if we have any sense, we shall never, in spite of reverses, give up the search. Self-love (properly understood) is the basis of all other love: it is the sole means for reaching out in a meaningful way to persons and things outside of ourselves.

* * *

See also Topic Nineteen, Nos. 2, 5, and 6;
Topic Twenty, No. 3.

CHAPTER FIVE

THOUGHTS ON SEX, LOVE, AND FRIENDSHIP

While rearranging my personal library, I one day discovered an old magazine article entitled "Sex and Love of God" by Bishop Sheen. It was typical of the many fine things this author has written over a period of years and very relevant to the needs of our times. The main point of the article was to show (as I hope to point out in this essay) that love is a matter both of giving and of receiving, and that it is simply a mistaken view of love to identify it on a physical level with sex.

For many years (and at a time when Freudian psychology had reached its zenith of popularity) it had been imagined that the repression of sex was the chief cause of many or most of the mental disorders from which people suffer. This error (and it is chiefly an error in *psychology*) was based on the false supposition that sex is not essentially different in man than it is in animals, i.e., that it is a biological power that demands biological fulfillment, that and nothing more. This supposition is false for the simple reason that sex in man is a *human* power subject to *human* needs, to *human* use, and to *human* control. To take any other view of the meaning of sex is to disregard the fact that sex has no real meaning for man as man except in the context of a genuine act of love. True enough, not all love is sexual love, but the point is that there is no sexual love either if the function of sex in man is reduced to the level of mere animal instinct.

But let us get back to a central point — namely, that the repression of sex is not the sole or chief cause of most mental disorders. As Fulton Sheen pointed out in his article there are six other possible causes: pride, covetousness, anger, envy, gluttony, and sloth. I do not mean to suggest here that the avoidance of sin is the sole or exclusive remedy for the treatment of mental disorders, but I would be quite willing to agree that there is a pretty close correlation between one type or another of sin — especially the root sin of selfishness (whatever its variant forms) and the many disorders of the mind which are so largely a characteristic of modern life. What matters here, however, is to know that "it is the *isolation* of the sex factor from the totality of human life which causes so many abnormalities and mental disorders." For an example, it is precisely in the mechanization of sex, in the attempt to pursue it apart from the context of a genuine love in marriage that the use of sex creates a split within the human personality and leads to all sorts of disorders.[1]

Needless to say, then, it is impossible for man to achieve his happiness by the pursuit of sex as an ultimate end in itself and as divorced from the overall purpose for which it is intended as a genuine expression of human love in marriage. But all of this brings us to the point of discussing the meaning of love itself, that is, in a yet larger context than that of sexual love. What does it mean for one person to love someone else? To this question there is no single answer

---

[1] In 1929 one author wrote in somewhat prophetic tones as follows: "For them [the Victorians] love, like God, demanded all sacrifices; but like Him, also, it rewarded the believer by investing all the phenomena of life with a meaning not yet analyzed away. We have grown used — more than they — to a Godless universe, but we are not yet accustomed to one which is loveless as well, and only when we have so become shall we realize what atheism really means," Joseph T. Krutch, *The Modern Temper* (New York: Harcourt, Brace and World, Inc., a Harvest Book, reprinted in 1956), p. 78.

that is satisfactory from every point of view. I venture to say, however, that the old definition of love which rather closely identifies it with a willing of what is good for another is as satisfactory as any other that one might project.

More than once St. Thomas has said that to love a person is nothing more than to will what is good for that person. Here no attempt is made to exclude from the act of loving whatever concrete and material gift might be chosen as an accompaniment and as an expression of the act of love. Far from it, as man is not a purely spiritual creature, the best way of knowing whether one person loves another is to know whether he "cares enough" to do something in behalf of the one he loves. We have every reason to be suspicious of the love of anyone who merely professes love without some kind of giving to accompany the act. For a young man to tell a young lady that he loves her it is necessary also for him to purchase gifts, to buy an engagement ring, to get serious sooner or later about marrying her. Otherwise love is an empty promise, and no true love at all. To love a person, then, is to will what is good for that other person, and to give some concrete expression of the good that one wills.

We have made a good start as to the meaning of love by placing love, not primarily in the emotions or feelings (important as these are) but in the will. This is a point of such central importance it should never be lost sight of. So many persons can involve themselves in useless scruples as to whether they really love another person or not, especially those who contemplate getting married. To suppose that in order really to love a person you must always get emotionally excited in that person's presence, that one's feelings must always be at a high pitch is to place an undue strain on one's love. This supposition too can easily lead to the mistake of supposing that because I cannot get excited about God at any particular moment, then I can't really be said to love God, which is a plain bit of nonsense that eats away at the conscience of many a scrupulous soul.

If, then, love is not primarily located in one's feelings and emotions but in the will, that is, in the will to do good for someone else, then the question as to whether I do or do not love a person becomes much easier to answer. The real practical test of one's love is to be gauged by one's habitual attitude and actions toward a given person. The hard-working mother of a family of children need have no scruples about her loving her children if she spends the better part of her life shopping for them, preparing their meals, getting them off to school, and helping them to organize their games, doing these tasks out of concern for them. There may be times when she loses her temper, when she *feels* that she would like to "resign," but none of these feelings, these occasional outbreaks of temper, in any way reflect on the real love that she has for her children from the oldest to the youngest of them. What I am trying to say here is that the test of real love lies in a willingness to do at least as much good for another person as one is habitually willing to do for himself.

In recent times philosophers have rightly emphasized — in the matter of love — the need for personal response, and I fully agree with them. Response, of whatever sort, is a basic sign, not only of love, but of life itself. If you step on a dead man's chest and get no response, then you *know* the man to be dead, and so too in the moral order: if you are generous, if you give the shirt off your back to a fellow human being, and you get no response, you begin to wonder what is wrong either with your shirt or with the man himself. Response is an essential part of the business of loving, but the question inevitably arises: "What *kind* of response?"

Take any beggar who is in need of a loaf of bread. Depending on your emotional makeup you may or may not *feel* sorry for the man, and the person who does *feel* sorry is responding in an emotional sort of way. Now the question is this: Does the person who so responds *really love* the beggar if in spite of his feelings he turns him down flat?

Hardly so, as it is in the act of giving that the real response of a love act genuinely lies. Contrariwise, your own response to the beggar may be minimally characterized by an emotional response to his needs. Yet in spite of this lack you nonetheless give him ungrudgingly what he asks for. Then clearly your love for the beggar is unquestioned and you have responded in the best sense of the word — by willing to do what is good for your fellowman. Herein, as I see it, lies the essence of all true love.

To sum up, we love a person when we respond to that which is closest to him, his personal needs. We respond to him when we make every attempt within our power toward the fulfillment of those needs. Thus a parent loves a child even while punishing him if it is punishment that the child most needs. We love an old lady if we help her across the street — whether she remembers to say thank you or not. A onetime miser loves his fellowman when he gives away that which lies closest to his heart, namely, his money. The test of loving lies in the giving of ourselves to another person in whatever way and by whatever means the circumstances of the moment require. The best way to pass this test is to follow the "golden rule" of doing for others the very thing we would most want others to do for us if we were in their place. To love is to will good for another. As one author puts it:

> Love is an active power in man; a power which breaks through the walls which separate man from his fellowmen, which unites him with others; love makes him overcome the sense of isolation and separateness, yet it permits him to be himself, to retain his integrity. In love the paradox occurs that two beings become one yet remain two.[2]

* * *

See also Topic Fourteen, No. 1;
Topic Sixteen, No. 9.

---

[2] Erich Fromm, *The Art of Loving* (New York: Harper & Row, 1956), pp. 20–21.

CHAPTER SIX

THE WISDOM OF ST. THOMAS: FOR AN EXAMPLE

Together with many of my contemporaries I feel that much ink has been spilled in academic controversies as to the pro's and con's of being "thomistic," "nonthomistic," and "antithomistic." For some persons "thomism" has been a rallying cry of a doctrine to be defended or attacked on all sides, of a kind of philosophy that should or should not be taught in our colleges and universities, a kind of "system" (which indeed it is not) that is regarded by some as being obsolete and by others (like myself) as having universal and perennial value. It is not the point of this essay to air any of these controversies except to say that the genuinely human wisdom of St. Thomas is often overlooked in the midst of them. Many of the persons who complain about St. Thomas have never read a line from his writings, have never really understood his philosophy, know little or nothing either of the sublimity of his wisdom or of the precision of many of his remarks. Even as a Christian philosopher I must confess that I myself have failed (over the years) to read St. Thomas as often and as regularly as I might only to discover when I come back to his masterful treatment of such topics as the *happiness of man* that I have been missing out on a much-needed diet.

By this I do not mean that St. Thomas has a monopoly on truth, but only that he has a way of saying things that is quite different from that of most contemporary thinkers.

True, the language he speaks is of a scholastic vocabulary that makes little appeal to the modern mind, yet his manner of saying things is seldom in the form of a casual or offhand remark. In a very broad and marvelously synthetic sense St. Thomas is (more than anything else) a man of principle, meaning that when he speaks his mind he does so in the context of some higher truth or principle that is part of the sweep of his vision.

For an example, take his treatment of The Good in his *Summa Contra Gentes* (Book III, Ch. 24). Every philosopher knows, of course, that goodness communicates itself. But catch something of the flavor in which St. Thomas handles this truth:

> The more perfect a thing's power, and the higher its degree of goodness, the more universal is its *desire* for good, and the greater the *range* of goodness to which its appetite and operation extend.[1]

To say merely that everything acts for the good is not enough for St. Thomas. Rather, he goes on to say that there is a *scale* of goodness in our actions: the more perfect *anything* is "the greater the *range* of goodness to which its appetite and operation extend." Reflect on this truth but a moment to see what it means.

It means first that imperfect things are restricted to their own private good. Thus, a person who is mean or selfish acts certainly for the good, but only for the good that he regards as beneficial to himself and not to other persons. He is preoccupied with his own affairs. Proportionately, as a person acts from a higher motive and for a higher good his *range of action* begins to expand. Such a person is concerned, not only with his private good, or the good of his immediate family, or of the local community, but even of the nation at large, or of the entire international community. If one chooses to give a theological twist to this principle, it be-

---

[1] *Summa Contra Gentes*, Book III, Ch. 24.

comes easy to see that God, being the Highest Good, extends His goodness — through divine action and power — to all other things. Nothing in the entire universe escapes the beneficent action of Divine Providence precisely because God is the Highest Good. Men too act in a manner similar to God when they extend the range of their activities to an ever widening circle of things and persons outside of themselves. Yet their range of action is always restricted by the limitations of their own nature and being.

I have given the above as a sample of the kind of reflection that is engendered by the wisdom of a mind that consistently sees things from above rather than from below, and this within the framework of philosophical principles that few persons ever bother to think about, including philosophers themselves. But let us take a further example of what represents at once the sweep of St. Thomas' mind and his ability to apply what he knows to man. The topic (*Summa Contra Gentes*, Book III, Ch. 25) is briefly this: *the weakness of the human mind with respect to its knowledge of God*. As Aquinas repeatedly insists, the human intelligence is like the "eye of the owl" which sees better in the darkness of material things than it does in the full light of day. God, in short, is supremely knowable in Himself, but not in relation to man.

Yet, granting this, St. Thomas does not back down on his principles to the point of giving up our knowledge of God as a lost cause. At this point many another philosopher might be tempted to say that man cannot know God at all in this life and that's an end to it. But this is not the position of Aquinas. On the contrary, he makes a strong stand to show that the knowledge, or better, the *understanding* of God is the end of *every* "intellectual substance," *including man*. True, man will never perfectly know God either in this life or, for that matter, in the Beatific Vision. But this is not to say that he cannot know God at all, since his very happiness lies in this very operation of his intelligence, which is his knowledge (*and* his love) of God. As St. Thomas puts it:

[Some] operations are not directed to some product, such as understanding and sensation. And since operations of this kind take their species from their *objects* . . . it follows that the more perfect the object of any such operation, the more perfect is the operation itself. Consequently, to understand the most perfect intelligible, *namely God*, is the most perfect operation . . . [which] is the end of *every* intellectual substance.[2]

Such high level wisdom can be taken by most persons only in small doses, but the substance of the argument is this: even though man's intelligence is the weakest of all (like the owl that sees in the darkness of material things), it is nonetheless ordered to God as its final and ultimate end. Accordingly, even a little knowledge of God in this life, however marked it may be by one kind or another of defect, is more perfect and valuable than the clearest knowledge we might have of "lower intelligibles," such as the bread we eat, the style of our homes, and the make of cars that we drive.

Much along the very same line of argument, St. Thomas goes on to show in the very same chapter that practical knowledge, unlike the speculative knowledge we might have of God, is not an end in itself. But again observe how he says it:

Now all practical sciences, arts and powers are lovable only for the sake of something else, since their end is not knowledge, but work. . . . For even playful actions, which seem to be done without any purpose, have some end due to them, namely that the mind may be relaxed, and that thereby we may afterward become more fit for studious occupations; or otherwise we should always have to be playing . . . and this is unreasonable.[3]

What a remarkably fine insight this — that not all actions are of equal value, since some of them are an end in themselves and others only a means to an end. Further, it is

---

[2] *Summa Contra Gentes*, Book III, Chap. 25.
[3] *Ibid.*

impossible in any case that there be no *ultimate* end or purpose for all of the operations we perform. And if this were
not so, it would hardly make any difference whether we
should be working or playing, or whether we should even be
doing anything at all. As the saying goes, *Sapientis est
ordinare* — "It is for the wise man to put order into things,"
and on this score each page of the *Summa* is a ready reminder
that St. Thomas was a wise man indeed.

So that the reader may know that the wisdom of Aquinas
is profoundly related to the business of everyday life, I close
this essay with a few scattered quotations on happiness as
they appear in Father Gilby's anthology[4] as follows:

> Only acts controlled by man through his reason and will
> are properly termed human: they proceed from deliberation.
> Others may be called acts of man, but they are not human
> in the specific sense of the term (*Summa Theologiae*, I–II,
> Q. 1, a. 1).

> Happiness is the great human good, the end to which all
> others are subordinate. It would be pernicious to a degree
> were happiness a matter of good luck, for then all other
> goods would be even more fortuitous, and so any deliberate
> attempt to lead a good life would go by the board (*Com-
> mentary on I Ethics, lecture 14*).

> A man need not always be preoccupied with his last end,
> any more than a wayfarer should always be thinking about
> the end of his journey with every step he takes.

P.S. This last remark and others like it are a reminder that
all men, insofar as they have a grain of common sense
within their intelligence, are in a broad sense "thomistic," whether they acknowledge it or not.

*   *   *

See also Topic Four, No. 6;
Topic Sixteen, No. 8;
Topic Twenty, No. 1.

---

[4] Thomas Gilby, O.P., *St. Thomas Aquinas: Philosophical Texts* (New York:
Oxford University Press, 1960), see Chap. XII, p. 263 ff.

CHAPTER SEVEN

INTELLECTUAL MODESTY AND THE PHILOSOPHER

To receive a letter from a former student is always a joy, but seldom more so than when that student is a warm personal friend. At present writing I find myself in correspondence with such a person now doing graduate work at New York University in social and political philosophy. My young friend has always done well at academic work, but not until he entered graduate work did his full potential come to the fore. Regardless, the question he asked in a recent letter was simply the question "What is philosophy?" and a difficult one it is. This question admits of no ready answer (except perhaps in early youth) and becomes all the more difficult to handle as one progresses in years and acquires an increased familiarity with the subject.

Actually a wide variety of answers is possible. For an example, to some persons philosophy *is* dialectics,[1] or the art of reaching probable conclusions when certainty is impossible; to others of more recent vintage, philosophy is the study of language and all the ambiguities to which it can lead; to others still, philosophy is "life," meaning that its sole or chief

---

[1] Some of the master dialecticians of our times are Mortimer Adler and Etienne Gilson, and Father Gerald Smith, S.J. perhaps as a close runner-up. Fortunately, however, none of these men would ever take such a narrow view of the scope of philosophy as to *identify* it with dialectics.

interest is the study of the problems of human life with particular reference to such practical fields as ethics and politics.

No doubt each of these answers contains a measure of
truth, but the situation that faces us here is the very same
one that faced Socrates in *Meno*: upon asking the question
"What is virtue?" Socrates was given such a variety of answers
as to become confused by them. Having looked for a definition of his subject (What is virtue?) he was attacked, as he
put it, by a "swarm of bees." In similar situations when we
ask "What is Philosophy?" we find there simply is no easy
answer to this question, nor is it possible to give a definition
that would satisfy all philosophers, to say nothing of the
majority of men.

But now to the point: however you choose to regard philosophy in an abstract sense, as a thing apart, what counts
most of all is for every aspiring philosopher to become a philosopher for himself. I stress this point (as I have stressed
it before) to forewarn the reader against the danger of regarding philosophy as one kind or another of *system*, a mistaken
conception that has been the bane of philosophers from the
time of Descartes (1596–1650) to the present day.

This intense passion for system is best evidenced perhaps
in the philosophy of Georg Wilhelm Hegel. No one, of
course, will deny that Hegel had many positive insights, such
as his insights into the evolutionary development of nature
and the use of dialectical method. Yet the mistake that he
made as a philosophical absolutist was to identify his own
vision of the truth (however enlarged) for the whole piece.
Indeed, he even regarded the previous development of philosophy as something merely preparatory to his own ideas on
God, man, and the universe. Given, then, such a pompous
conception as this, a reaction was bound to set in, which it
did in the form of Kierkegaard's criticism of Hegel as *The*
Philosopher. Kierkegaard's point was to show that no man
(whatever his genius) ever has the right to regard himself (or
to allow others so to regard him) as *The* Supreme Genius

of Philosophy, in whom all subsequent development is reduced to the mere filling in of details.

But let me return to my basic point that every philosopher *should* become a philosopher for himself. By this I mean, *not* that philosophers should isolate themselves from the influence of other men, but precisely that

1. They should develop their own insights (and not rely slavishly on any one system of thought), and

2. They should never mistake the sum total of their own insights for the whole of the truth.

Obviously, the mind of the philosopher, like the mind of anyone else, has stringent limitations, and it is well to mark off the boundary lines of one's intellectual achievements. *No one can ever claim for himself a complete possession of all philosophical truth.*

It is this very last point that raises the question as to the need for a virtue that many persons fail to possess and can only emulate in others, namely, intellectual modesty. By this I do not mean mediocrity or indifference in the face of intellectual values, but rather what some existential philosophers have called "humility before being." On this subject I quote from a philosopher friend of mine who speaks thus concerning St. Thomas' estimation of the virtue of modesty:

> Aquinas locates *modestia* in the scheme of the virtues as something akin to temperance: it is a virtue which has to do with regulating and restraining the less powerful tendencies in human nature . . . such as those that have to do with man's pursuit of knowledge . . . surely it is superficial to seek for knowledge *unless we have made a prior estimation of the overall impact the search for knowledge will have on our lives.* Putting this view of scholarship into more modern terms, it might run something like this: the exercise of one's academic freedom is subject to prior moral restraint. *The search after knowledge, no matter how courageous and demanding, must at bottom be a tempered one.*[2]

2 John R. Klopke, C.PP.S., "The Modesty of Thomistic Metaphysics," *Proceedings of the American Catholic Philosophical Association*, Vol. XXXVII (1963), pp. 204–205.

The above words may be a bit puzzling to a person who regards knowledge as an absolute good, but the point is that knowledge is only one of life's values, and the measure of one's knowledge should be proportioned to the limited capacities of one's own mind.[3] As the Romans once said: "*Sumite materiam aequam viribus*," or in American slang, "Don't tackle anything that lies beyond your own strength."

It is true, of course, that the human intellect is in potency to the knowledge of all things, and it is *only* too true that the "sin" of most men is a "sin" of defect, which is to say, a *failure* to develop their intellectual potential. Yet for those who are tempted to intellectual pride it would seem quite wise to develop one's knowledge

1. In a measure and at a pace that would avoid excessive straining, and
2. In a measure that involves due reflection upon the gains that have been made.

Continually to widen the expanse of one's knowledge without the pause that refreshes the soul impresses me as being a sort of *avaritia* that is worse in some respects than that of the miser who accumulates large sums of money without regard to the purpose for which it exists.

But let me return at this point to the student I mentioned at the beginning of this essay. In answer to his question "What is philosophy?" I penned the following letter:

Dear Tom,

I trust your courses are coming along well. Keep up the ferment, but don't strain too hard. Now and then give yourself a good solid dose of distraction. New York should be the ideal place to find some relief from the purely intellectual life.

---

[3] A similar point is made (regarding the spiritual life) by Father Teilhard de Chardin in *The Divine Milieu*: "In the spiritual life, as in all organic processes, everyone has his *optimum* and it is just as harmful to go beyond it as not to attain it." In a word, there is a kind of intellectual and spiritual ambition (as a purely selfish affair) that all persons, especially those who are creative, should seek to avoid. Pierre Teilhard de Chardin, *The Divine Milieu*, trans. by B. Wall (New York: Harper & Row, 1960), pp. 74–75.

This question as to the exact nature of philosophy is as much puzzling to me after all these years even as it is to you now. Philosophy itself is an analogical term meaning at one time a way of life, at another a method of rational inquiry, or even (at times) some kind or another of mysticism. I am convinced, however, that in its purest form and at its highest level of achievement philosophy is metaphysical insight by way of causality leading upward to an imperfect knowledge of God. Yet here I must hasten to add that philosophy must include as well such practical subjects as ethics, politics, philosophy of art, of history, and all the rest.

No doubt it is impossible to get unanimous agreement as to the nature of philosophical thought. Even so, the great modern error (behind all the variant opinions) is the failure to respect the *integral nature* of man and *all* of his human experience. Take, for an example the preoccupation with the problem of knowledge as such. I do not deny, of course, that *knowledge is a problem* but the more a person multiplies and refines his negative doubts, the deeper the hole that he digs to the point that all perspective is lost. Given this loss of perspective, there is only one way to run for escape — toward some kind or another of skepticism, positivism, or agnosticism. What is needed is a firm grasp of reality at the outset, a grasp that one unswervingly maintains regardless of any difficulties, doubts, or problems that may arise. To hold to this line of approach is to walk the path of a philosophical realism which in the end is the only guarantee against all forms of philosophical insanity.

Personally, I have arrived at a stage of development in my own intellectual life where I feel a great need for simplicity, for a closer contact with nature and my fellowman. Though I am getting away from your original question, I think that the problem of modern man is not at all a problem of the need for more and more introspection,[4] but of the need for

---

[4] As a *notandum* to this point in my letter, I have subsequently come across some interesting points in the philosophy of Josiah Royce. According to Royce true self-consciousness is not attained by an introspective analysis of oneself. An individual can peer into himself only so far and then he reaches a darkness. He becomes confused by the many contradictory forces within himself. He sees many possible selves and he is at a loss to choose a direct plan of life. Royce claims that at this point the individual must get outside of himself and willfully extend himself to the community. It is

a certain kind of therapy to help restore him to his more normal human condition. This is not to take an antirational or irrational view of man but to recognize that man is a delicate balance of a variety of elements some of them rational, others not, but it is part of the work of the philosopher to know where this balance lies. As to the vocation of the philosopher himself I am sure that it has something to do with the need for all of us becoming in some important respects like children again.

I would suggest that intellectual modesty is a virtue that suits all men, but particularly those for whom intellectual pride is an occupational hazard. The vocation of the philosopher, then, is always that of one who is *seeking* the truth with a sense of humility before being. To follow this path is to pursue authentic being with a sense of unwavering fidelity to the truth of that which lies both within and outside of ourselves.

*   *   *

See also Topic Two, No. 8;
Topic Fourteen, Nos. 5–6.

---

in and through his participation in the life of the community that the individual truly finds himself.

CHAPTER EIGHT

FROM DESCARTES TO SARTRE: A BIRD'S-EYE VIEW

It is impossible for modern man to know himself without also knowing his historical antecedents, and not the least of these antecedents is the development of philosophical thought in the past 350 years. What I shall do, therefore, in this essay is to provide the reader with a sketch — whose value lies in knowing that a real continuity exists in modern thought from the time of Descartes to the present day.

Begin, then, with Descartes in the first half of the seventeenth century. Descartes's philosophy, like any other, was inspired by a fundamental motive — which in this particular case was to reestablish philosophy itself on such a firm, unmistakable basis that no one in the future could ever question its value or use. At the time of Descartes, scholastic philosophy had fallen into disrepute, and although Descartes himself had been trained by the Jesuits, he was very little satisfied with the training he had received. On top of all this he was impressed with the advancing growth of the sciences and had a strong desire to defend philosophy against such skeptical thinkers as Montaigne. But where was he to begin and how would he find a method of certainty that no one could possibly deny? Interestingly enough, Descartes did not begin his philosophy with an external world taken as such because it was altogether too easy, he felt, to be misled by one's senses. Instead, he chose to begin *introspectively* by examining the very contents of the mind. The principle Descartes sought as the initiating point of all philosophical knowledge was some incontrovertible truth that no one could question or deny: This principle he found and expressed in his now famous dictum *Cogito ergo sum* ("I think therefore I am"). Whatever the significance of this principle let it be clearly understood that Descartes placed his fundamental trust, not in the power of his senses, but in the power of his reason to know the truth as it lies within consciousness itself.

Though Descartes himself tried to reestablish the world on a realistic basis by reasoning upward to God and then back to the world of things, there were some men in Britain who did not. Take Bishop George Berkeley for an example: Berkeley certainly believed in the existence of *God*, but the problem with him was that he was far less convinced of the material world itself — for in his philosophy *Esse est percipi*, which is to say that *to be* is nothing other than *to be perceived*. As one wag put it, "If I don't see you, you don't *be* you." The significance of Berkeley's philosophy is precisely that it involves a yet deeper retreat into the inner recesses of the mind and a complete withdrawal from the world.

In Berkeley's philosophy, then, there is no question of the *dominance* of mind over matter, but of the reduction of matter itself to the subjective *states of one's mind*.[1] What matters here is to know that the central focus of modern philosophy through Berkeley, and after him Hume, is not on the world as such, but on the self-conscious pursuit of ideas, images, and impressions. In Hume this approach to philosophy reaches a climactic point of development in which the very reality of the ego itself — to say nothing of the

---

[1] In the next chapter I shall point out that the acosmism of Berkeley had a profound effect both in England and in America on the puritanical devaluation of the world.

human soul — is methodologically swept away and denied. Whereas modern philosophy begins with Descartes in an attempt to make ideas clear and certain, it ends up with Hume in a state of confusion and doubt.

This unhappy state of affairs could not have lasted for long, and the happy day of the restoration of philosophy had seemingly dawned with the advent of the great German philosopher, Immanuel Kant. Awakened from his dogmatic slumbers, as he himself puts it, by the pan-phenomenalism of Hume, Kant attempted within the framework of his system to reestablish a bridge between mind and thought on the one hand, and reality on the other. Though his motivation was sound, the results in terms of a realistic philosophy were meager, since the metaphysics of Kant was a radical reassertion of our inability to know the world as it is in itself. Instead of restoring reality to mind, Kant did no more than restore the *appearances* of the world. The world as it exists out there — the real world — forever remains hidden from mind, and in such a philosophy to know is not to establish a living contact between the mind and the things, but to *impose* on a world of appearances the forms — the *a priori* forms — of one's own thoughts taken as such. Again, the basic orientation of thought, though not purely subjective, derives its basic principle of order and unity from within the mind itself. *It is the mind itself which imposes meaning on the meaningless world of things,* leaving the person in a complete state of ignorance as to the ultimate nature of God, man, and the world.

But here let us take a deep breath since the air one breathes from Descartes through Kant is like that in the earliest model submarines — which were lacking in oxygen tanks. In the language of traditional metaphysics we have cut ourselves off from the roots of being which alone give life to the mind. The mind of modern man during this classical period of philosophy is a mind starved for the oxygen of the real world by which it is surrounded but from which it is hermetically sealed.

But let us go on with our story before we make any attempt to see how it applies to the plight of contemporary man. The story after Kant continues with Hegel's bold and noble attempt to get man outside of himself, away from the subjective states of his own consciousness, of his own mental categories into the objective realm of the real world. To the eternal credit of Hegel — however unsuccessful he might otherwise have been — it must be said that he as much as any of the modern philosophers attempted to restore metaphysics to its rightful status as the core of all philosophical thinking, and this through the use of a dynamic evolutionary method that had later been taken over in the dialectic of Karl Marx. The problem with Hegel, however, was that his attempt to restore metaphysics, although sufficiently objective in scope and motivation, was in the form of an objective *idealism*, and the problem that arose from Hegel's preoccupation with the Absolute was the diminishing emphasis on the reality of the individual, the significance of the person, and the meaning of human freedom.

Resentment to this sort of thinking was bound to set in and set in it did in the form of the rejection of Hegel and all of his philosophical works and pomps. This exorcism of Hegel — and with it all academic and systematic philosophy — was conducted quite modestly and effectively by a deeply religious thinker from Denmark, Søren Kierkegaard. This humble Dane stood in radical opposition to anything that absorbed the individual — whether the monster in question be in the form of the organized Church of Denmark or in the form of any systematic philosophy that claimed to have an enlightened vision of the truth. It was Kierkegaard's protest against the pretensions of a philosophy that rode the high seas that marked the beginnings of the existentialist movement as we know it today.

The subsequent development of contemporary thought took place in one or the other of two general directions, that is, in the direction of logic or in the direction of philosophy of life. According to the first direction, philosophy became, as it were, the handmaid of logic or, even worse, its obsequious slave. Reason, in short, had become even further isolated from the domain of reality than it ever had been in the times of Descartes, Berkeley, and Hume. The culmination of this new movement took place under the inspiration of the now famous Vienna Circle in the form of *logical positivism* as we know it today. In such a system reason withdraws into an escape hatch of logical systems and relations, and bars the door to the all-important problems of human life.

At the opposite end of the pole and in the direction of the *life-philosophies*, the philosophies of the concrete in the nineteenth and twentieth centuries, we find *pragmatism, communism*, and *existentialism*.[2] Few of these last-mentioned philosophies have even the remotest concern with the questions of logic, because they are intimately, even passionately, devoted to the problems of life, the assumption being that logic has little or nothing to do with life. On this point Karl Marx put his finger on the spirit of the movement by saying that previous philosophers only thought about reality whereas the whole point of the matter was to change it, and change it he did.

At this point of the essay I am far less concerned in directing the reader's attention toward these life philosophies for their own sake as to illustrate a principle or starting point from which each of them stems. In the older metaphysics of Augustine, Aquinas, and Bonaventure the problem for man is the problem of the discovery of meaning in a world which fundamentally makes sense because it was created by God. In the new life-philosophies of the past 100 years —

---

[2] Outstanding examples of these philosophers of the concrete are: Schopenhauer, Nietzsche, Bergson, James, and Dewey.

in such disparate philosophies as those of Schopenhauer, Marx, James, and Sartre — the world that confronts man is precisely a world which for various reasons does *not* make sense. It is a world bequeathed to contemporary man by the categorical imperative of Immanuel Kant on a take it or leave it basis, and if you take it, then it is you who must impose your own meaning on the world. The world of the concrete philosophers is a real world, indeed, but it is also one that is drained of any inherent intelligibility of its own, or, in the more radical language of the avant-garde existentialists, a world of absurdity; and now we have gone full cycle: from the certainty of Descartes, to the doubt of Hume, to the criticism of Kant, and to the absurdity of *some* of the neo-existentialists.

Given this situation, the problem for man now is not to establish on epistemological grounds the existence of the world, but to carve out a meaning for himself. As James had said, "God exists for me if God makes a difference in my life" — whether any actual God exists or not. Not every thinker, however, was as romantic in spirit as William James, for the day would dawn for Sartre to declare that the existence of God is impossible if it is possible for man to be free. Here, then, lies the central issue at the heart of all modern thought — whether *there is or is not any objective meaning in the world.* If so, then, a true metaphysics is possible, an ethics is possible, and it is possible to draw up a true philosophy of man. If not, then none of these traditional disciplines has any more value than the smoke that one can blow from his pipe.

To sum up, the world of contemporary philosophers is one of considerable bewilderment as to the meaning of the world and as to the meaning of human life. It is here precisely where the greatest challenge lies to the Christian philosopher. Since the problem after Kant is man's failure to *discover* — and not merely to *impose* meaning on reality and life — it is here that the Christian philosopher must begin, namely, with the discovery of an objective world of reality outside of himself and of himself as an integral part of that world. Mark well the tensions inherent in contemporary man's view of himself: having denied an objective world of reality outside of that which is measurable by scientific means, he has lost sight of the real world of ethical and religious values, and with this ontological loss he has suffered no end from a distorted image of his own nature and destiny.

The great problem, then, is to liberate man from the overweening influence of a psychologism that has entrapped man in feelings of anxiety, neurotic guilt, and psychotic confusion. Never has it been more apparent — in the light of the helplessness of modern man to liberate himself from his own ego — that the fundamental need is for man to rediscover who he is and what he is for — other than in terms of the pursuit of sexual freedom, economic wealth, and the cult of a misguided leisure which, far from removing the conflicts of life, serves only to intensify them.

Psychologism in its very essence consists in an attempt to create meanings where there is the need to discover them, and on the negative side it consists in the fallacy of genetic reductionism: because there is a tendency in man to serve "some sort of God" the very meaning of "God" is *nothing more* than a projection of the subconscious, or, as in Freud, the erection of a father image, which has no more than psychological roots. Here lies the heart of modern subjectivism, and the only way to cure it is from the root — by a reexamination of the *metaphysical* basis of that which *is* — outside of and distinct from the mind. Whereas psychologism begins and ends in the ego, metaphysical realism begins with the senses and carries man upward toward an enlightened vision of himself and the world around him.

Every person alive has a vested interest in knowing what his true nature is as a human person, and one of the great

misfortunes of our times is that modern sophistry has obscured man's fundamental vision of himself. It is this very
lack of vision which is one of the chief roots of the many
tensions and conflicts that lie at the root of contemporary
life. To compensate for this myopia what is needed is a
realism in psychology that goes beyond either a purely
rational or a purely empirical approach to the subject, a
realism that derives its meaning from the world *as God
created it, and not as man reconstructs it according to his
own self-created myths.* The great myth of contemporary
life is not the so-called myth of religion or of an absolutist
system of ethics, but the myth that man can liberate himself
by means of a freedom that knows no goals outside of itself.
Whereas virtue was the end of a much earlier Greek society,
freedom has become dominant in our own — as though man
by the creative use of his freedom could achieve for himself
any prescribed goals he might choose.

The *task of the Christian philosopher,* therefore, is not
to create new worlds of his own in competition with the
false myths of modern society but to restore man to his
rightful status as a person who is of more intrinsic worth
than all the technology in the world. There is the need in the
first place for a recovery, a redeeming of the senses, and
this means that modern man must be reeducated to perceive
things as a child again. Technology and pragmatism have reduced the value of the senses to the sheer lower level of
their biological utility, whereas the Christian philosopher
must help modern man to know that the senses have a contemplative value of their own.

Lest it be thought, however, that knowledge begins and
ends on the level of the senses the Christian philosopher
must reassert the *value of human intelligence* in terms of
the operations of the laws that are proper to its own intelligible necessities, and here again we see the need for
an emergence from psychologism (which regards the intellect

as no more than a useful tool) into a view of the intelligence that guarantees its contact with the real world.[3]

In closing this essay I must stress the point that the value of Christian philosophy depends in large measure on the personal outlook of the Christian philosopher himself. For a Christian philosopher to close the door to a yet higher wisdom is merely to pave the way to a new type of Averroism, which is no more than a sign of intellectual pride. A Christian philosopher who is a philosopher and nothing more is untrue to his Faith, and a Christian philosopher who is untrue to his faith is no Christian at all. The great need, therefore, is to cultivate a kind of philosophical thinking that moves freely within the orders both of reason and of faith.

*　　*　　*

See also Topic Three, No. 3;
Topic Eleven, Nos. 1 and 2;
Topic Twelve, No. 5.

---

[3] The problem is to extricate man from the web of his own illusions and myths: What he needs is a kind of philosophy that will help him to rediscover objective meaning in himself and in the world. This means he must develop the capacity to understand something of the hidden realities that underlie the appearances of sensible things.

CHAPTER NINE

THE AMERICAN CONFLICT AND THE NEED FOR AN INCARNATIONAL PHILOSOPHY

Several times over a period of years I have had occasion to teach a course entitled *Introduction to American Philosophy*. The subject matter of this course is fascinating for a number of reasons, but especially because it introduces one to the split in our American culture between pragmatism and idealism. As I shall have more to say in other parts of this volume on the nature of pragmatism, I shall restrict myself here to a basic consideration of idealism. In fact, idealism was the *first* philosophy to make its appearance on American shores, and the first group of idealists were the Puritans.

As to the background of Puritan idealism, this much is clear: it is a direct carry-over of Berkeley's idealism, which may be summed up in not too many words as follows: (1) nothing exists independently of mind, and (2) the very existence of the material world itself consists in its being perceived (*esse est percipi*). The underlying principle of Berkeley's philosophy (as it was earlier of Descartes and Locke) is that the mind is restricted to the possession of its own ideas. This principle leads to a certain type of acosmism,[1]

---

[1] Given the supposition that I know nothing other than my own ideas, it follows by logical consequence that the material world has no other existence than a mental one — whether in God's mind or in our own. Further, insofar as the idealism of Jonathan Edwards and others was a direct carryover from the idealism of Berkeley, it involved a downgrading, a denigration of the world of matter, and an exultation of the world of spirit.

a denial of the world and its values, such as is found in the thinking of the great Puritan idealist of seventeenth-century America, Jonathan Edwards.

Take, for an example, the following quotation from Edwards:

> If we had only the sense of Seeing, we should not be as ready to conclude the visible world to have been an existence independent of perception as we do. . . . But we know that the objects of this sense, all that the mind views by Seeing, are merely mental Existences . . . all material existence is only idea.[2]

No need here to go into a deeper understanding of the acosmism of Berkeley and Edwards except to say that acosmism both in its real and etymological sense means quite literally a "denial of the world." Paradoxically it was in the spirit of this type of thinking that American philosophy began, even as men were cutting down forests and building homes. More specifically, the acosmism of the Puritan divines means that human effort was a matter of no ultimate concern. All that did matter was for the pioneer to lead a good moral life in the hope of saving his soul. Most discouraging of all, however, was the predestinationist doctrine that the very salvation of one's soul was entirely in the hands of God, in the sense that nothing that man himself could do would ultimately make a difference. Human freedom, in other words, as a factor by which man could choose for himself (with God's grace) the pathway to salvation was denied. Men — which is to say — some men — were predestined to be saved, and others, no matter how hard they tried, were not. In short, the Puritan denial of the world and its values was accompanied with the denial of the value of human nature as such.[3]

---

[2] From Jonathan Edwards' "Notes on the Mind" as found in Mueldner-Sears-Schlabach, *The Development of American Philosophy* (Boston: Houghton Mifflin Co., 1960), p. 9.

[3] Thus the overall picture we get is the distressing one of a fundamental acosmism combined with an antihumanism that could only repel the person who stood for the defense of the rights of man.

Little wonder in the light of all this that the spirit of the American enlightenment (in the eighteenth century and beyond) was to blossom out in bitter opposition to the whole Puritan movement, that is, against its nihilistic view of the world, against its spiritualistic psychology, and against its complicated system of ethical and religious taboos. Read, if you will, almost any page of the writings of Jefferson, Franklin, and Paine, and you will find more than a superficial reaction to any kind of religion that bases itself on supernaturally revealed truth. As a matter of fact, most of the men in the revolutionary period were deists who wanted a minimum of dogma and a maximum of freedom to assert their own ability to *change* a world which to them was *most real*, and to change it *for the better*. In the spirit of Benjamin Franklin, "The Lord helps those who help themselves," and this spirit represents the beginning of the subsequent development of naturalism and pragmatism in America.

The basic conflict, then, in the shaping up of the "American mind" has been a failure to reconcile the goals of a supernaturally revealed faith with the goals of a secular culture. Whereas the religious posture of the Puritan was one of withdrawal from the world, the attitude of the men who shaped our economic and political institutions was one of total commitment to the world and its values, and joined to this commitment was a rejection, however implicit at times, of the older forms of supernatural religion. *The most tragic aspect of this conflict is that it has never been satisfactorily resolved.* Unhappily, too many persons have rejected all religion, and more recently all belief in God, on the basis of their own identification of the spirit of religion with the spirit of what is now known to be an outmoded form of idealism.

The problem, then, is to get people to reflect on the need, not only for what has been called an incarnational theology, but even more fundamentally an incarnational metaphysics, an incarnational psychology, and an incarnational ethics. In the balance of this essay I should like the reader to consider each of these in its turn with a view toward a better understanding of the means of resolving the conflict I mentioned but a moment ago.

Let us first direct our attention to "incarnational metaphysics." Fundamentally, what I mean is this: a view of the world and of all reality that is thoroughly grounded in the vast realm of human experience and one that forever remains faithful to that experience. By an incarnational metaphysics I do not mean one that fails to transcend experience — as indeed it must in order to be a true metaphysics — but one that does not end up with a denial of the world. It is the very opposite, if you will, of the acosmism of George Berkeley, Jonathan Edwards, and Ralph Waldo Emerson. In yet more positive terms an incarnational metaphysics is one which recognizes and in practice is faithful to the inherent value and dignity of all finite being and of every finite operation that man can perform. It is a metaphysics which looks outward to the world of things and other persons, and not inward to the introspective realm of my own thoughts taken as such and the world of my own imaginings. It is a metaphysics which, though fully accounting for all that goes on in the realm of true subjectivity, is based on an objective order of things.

Considering the novelty of the term, I realize that there is need for a much greater precision as to what an incarnational metaphysics includes and what it denies, but my sole concern here is to characterize its fundamental spirit. What I have in mind here is the kind of metaphysics that will help to bridge the gap, so to speak, between metaphysics and science, metaphysics and human experience, including human artistic experience, and most important of all between metaphysics and religion, even religious mystical experience.[4] As

---

[4] My assertion of the need for an incarnational metaphysics is in no way intended to discredit the permanent and inherent value of the metaphysics of the schools, least of all the metaphysics of St. Thomas. What I would

for the spirit of such a metaphysics I conceive it to be the very opposite of the spirit of rationalism that prevailed during the period of decadent scholasticism and the spirit of the German idealisms both before and after the time of Kant. Indeed, given the aberrant forms of metaphysics such as they have developed in the past, it is little wonder that the very word "metaphysics" conjures up a bad taste in the minds of many.

Yet none of this need be so, and the great truth is that a denial of metaphysics in any of its older forms — either good or bad — inevitably results in some new attempt to reinstate metaphysics through the back door by a different name. Rather than see this happen, I would much prefer that metaphysics be reinstated, not only as the science of reality "in general," but as the science of a reality that is true to every aspect of human experience from the lowest to the highest. Apropos of the American scene, it is time for American thought to become impregnated with the fundamental laws of things as they are, and not as man himself imagines them to be through the creation of his own false myths and images.

All of what I am saying is in the nature of a plea for a reawakening of a genuine metaphysics which is sensitive to the values of the society in which we live. On this point,

---

promptly reject, however, is the opinion that metaphysics, even a sound one, can be true to itself if it ignores what Maritain has called the present *state* of mankind, which is to say the actual conditions of the culture in which we live.

From this point of view I feel that too many thomists have isolated themselves from the culture in which they live, and have in many ways allowed their metaphysics to become for them barren and sterile. To use the language of a Trappist friend of mine, thomistic metaphysics is for many scholars, especially in the United States, a "deep freeze" metaphysics, that is, a philosophy that has cut itself off from the roots of contemporary existence. Little do such persons who cling to the philosophy of the past as past intend to impregnate their philosophy, their metaphysics, with issues of present-day relevance, giving the impression to most outsiders (and a false one it is, indeed) that *their* philosophy is no more than an outmoded form of idealism!

In the best sense of the word, then, thomistic metaphysics is or can become incarnational but only if it becomes alive in the minds of men who are aware of the conflicts of the culture in which they live.

however, I am realistic enough to acknowledge that this good thing will never come about if metaphysicians forever remain in their shells. If the metaphysical realist takes an attitude of indifference toward nature and man, he does so at the risk of his own obsolescence. Accordingly, it is necessary, on the one hand, for the metaphysician to develop a cosmic outlook and to affirm in unmistakable terms the value of modern science and technology. On the other, he must learn fully to appreciate the insights of modern psychology, the meaning of human *Angst*, man's fundamental need for religion, his will to meaning, and all the rest. To give direction to modern man, the metaphysician must know *whom* he directs.

Earlier in this essay I have spoken of the need as well both for an "incarnational" psychology and an "incarnational" ethics. Let me expand on the use of both of these terms. By an incarnational psychology I mean one which takes fully into account the psychosomatic nature of all of our human experience. The Puritans were wrong in treating man as though he were no more than a displaced spirit that happens for a time to be ensconced in a body; equally wrong were those evolutionists who claimed along purely naturalistic lines that man is no more than a product of the evolutionary development of nature, as though there were no such thing as the reality of the human soul. The one view exaggerates the transcendence of man over nature and the other altogether denies it. A truly incarnational psychology is one that recognizes man for what he actually is in terms both of the lower and higher parts of his nature and seeks to subordinate the lower (such as the passions, sense appetites, and so on) to the higher (such as reason and will).

As for an incarnational ethics I mean one which neither makes impossible demands on human nature nor relegates man to the tyranny of his own animalistic drives. The mistake of the Puritans was precisely the first: to ask man to behave like a spirit because they thought that he *was* one indeed. The mistake of the behaviorists was to attribute everything to the work of stimulus and response so that man had no effective moral or religious control over his environment. By contrast, a genuine incarnational ethics is one that proposes for man an *ideal* of conduct, but an ideal that is consonant with his total nature as a fun-loving, art-making, rational animal.

Here, then, lies the way out of the dilemma in which American culture has been rooted for so many years: to work toward the development of what in America at least is a "new" philosophy, but of a philosophy which is both "ever old, ever new," in short, a perennial philosophy. Lest it be thought, however, that in this author's view philosophy itself is the cure for all the evils of our day, I should say that philosophy is never a substitute for religion.[5] Rather, the ultimate resolution of the conflict in American culture between idealism and secularism should be effected through a spirit of religion rightly considered, adequately conceived, and thoroughly practiced. Even so, it may yet take a long time before all men are united in faith, and it is more than likely that before they do this, they will first be united, if they are united at all, in the common bond of their humanity. In the meantime no time will be wasted in any attempt to work toward the dream of a united humanity in some such terms as were spelled out by the American philosopher, Josiah Royce, in his conception of the beloved community and more recently by the great French Jesuit, Father Teilhard de Chardin, in his own conception of all men working toward a common good.

*   *   *

See also Topic Twelve, No. 4;
Topic Fourteen, No. 2.

---

[5] As Gilson points out, Justin Martyr in his search for a true philosophy was looking for something more than a philosophy when he finally did decide to embrace the Christian Faith.

CHAPTER TEN

EXISTENTIALISM AND THE SPIRIT OF GABRIEL MARCEL

All too often name tags in philosophy become rallying points of a doctrine or idea that must be defended or attacked, and whenever a situation like this prevails, the open-minded desire for truth has a hard time surviving. For reasons of this sort, I suspect, most "existentialists" shy away from the use of this and similar terms, and Gabriel Marcel, one of the finest Christian thinkers of our day, is no exception. In the present essay I have no desire to give a complete panorama either of "existentialism" as a philosophy or of the thought of Marcel. My intent is rather to initiate the reader to the spirit of this new mode of thought and to touch on some of the themes of the "Christian existentialism" of Marcel.

Existentialism is a much-abused term, and the first thing to do is to distinguish between "existentialism" as a philosophy and what in literary circles is known as the "existential revolt." This latter semipopular movement is impossible to define since it is many things wrapped into one. From one aspect, it represents a growing dissatisfaction, especially among the youth, with certain prevailing cultural ideals, such as the cult of conformity and (together with it) the worship of the fruits of technology. It represents a reaction to the hollow commitment of previous generations to ideals — either secular or religious — that were never fully lived up to. It represents certain new forms of poetry, art and drama of the shock-type variety, literature of the sort which — however disjointed its language may be — is meant to make people return to their wits.

The existential revolt (as it exists both in Europe and in America) is the semipopular predecessor of a movement which has not yet become strong enough to find full philosophical development. It is a movement that is closely aligned in spirit with such thinkers as Jean-Paul Sartre and Albert Camus. It is a movement of protest, an outcry of human freedom against the depersonalization, the dehumanization of man. It is an attempt to restore, in however unorthodox fashion, some appreciation for the realm of mystery, especially that of man's own being. Too often, however, it is characterized by a sort of worldly asceticism — as that of the Zen Buddhists — an asceticism which unfortunately fails to lead to any real illuminative way. The spirit of this revolt may be summed up as a protest against conformity and against any attempt to make man a robot. It is a protest against the hypocrisy that pledges itself to a set of ideals and then fails to live up to them. It is a revolt that is distrustful of the kind of pure relationism which claims to know in some facile way all the answers to life's problems, without any commensurate effort to solve those problems on the part of those who make such a claim.

So much for the "existential revolt." As for the meaning of "existentialism" as a philosophy, here again it is hazardous to make any generalized statements, since the name itself is a slippery one. This much, however, should be said: many of today's "existentialists" are far more acute in diagnosing man's problems than they are competent to provide the positive remedies that are needed to solve them. Some of the current existentialisms, at any rate, are philosophies of crisis that point up the need — usually through literary channels — of a radical reexamination of man's situation in the world, so that with the notable exception of Gabriel Marcel they are often too pessimistic in their outlook (especially Sartre) to suppose that any real happiness is available to man either in this life or in the next.

Clearly, one of the great advantages of existentialism as

a new mode of thinking is that it has helped to rid man of some of the myths and chimeras of the past, like the religion of progress that prevailed during the height of the Victorian era. Contemporary man — at least the most reflective of his kind — to the extent that he is honest with himself is no longer content with the ephemeral modes of activity that gave a measure of escapist satisfaction to an earlier generation whose sense of values was sunk no deeper than the roots of his sensible experience. Unfortunately, however, there has been too much emphasis on the "absurdity" of human existence (witness the theater of the absurd) and the consequent feeling of "nausea" that is the result of this heightened sense of absurdity.

As a counterbalance for this sense of absurdity, it is a good thing that man, including contemporary man, has, in a manner of speaking, a built-in mechanism for rejecting too heavy a diet of nausea a la Jean-Paul Sartre; this is to say that there comes a time when he wants to bounce back to good health. Happily, there exists in most persons enough of a reservoir of good sense to enable them to know that shock treatment, administered in excessive amounts, can have the paradoxical effect of dulling one's sensibilities instead of awakening them to new and creative efforts, and it is for reasons of this sort that existentialism, if it is to survive as a valid mode of philosophical inquiry, should pave the way for new and different ways of thinking that lead to positive results.[1]

The tragedy, then, of so much of contemporary existentialism is that it sees only the crisis side of human experience. It is so deeply immersed in the categories of anguish and

---

[1] Marcel, for an example, in a speech delivered at De Paul University in the fall of 1963, made this highly important point: "It is a serious mistake to consider anguish or despair as existential categories par excellence to the exclusion of the more positive experiences." It is this more positive outlook that I take to be one of the essential conditions to the growth of existential philosophy, a condition that is essential to its own confrontation with authentic being. A too highly negative outlook that stresses only the gloomy side of life can only lead one back to the pessimism of Hobbes, Schopenhauer, and Nietzsche, or at best to the development of some form of neo-jansenism.

despair that it fails to point upward to the illuminating heights of a higher wisdom that is shut off from its eyes. It is true, of course, that the experience of the pessimistic existentialist is genuine and authentic enough, but such an experience needs to be utilized and directed toward a true sense of human fulfillment, and the problem here is that of being caught up in the middle of a crisis without any intimation of the finality or the end to which that crisis might lead. For this reason, too, pessimistic existentialism is only a partial and limited experience which cuts itself off from the best and most authentic part of reality, and which in its moment of crisis and agony fails to see the ray of light that will yet shine through the cave. As a poet once said, "Hope springs eternal in the human breast," though unhappily to the minds of some existentialists there is neither hope, nor what William James has called the "will to believe."

If what I have said is true, it would appear that from a Christian point of view one of the great intellectual needs of our times is that of a Christian existentialism that sees all things in a proper balance. Such an existentialism would involve: (1) a proper assessment both of the good and bad points of the culture in which we live; (2) an understanding of the reasons for the failure of Christians to respond morally, spiritually, artistically, and intellectually to the challenges of our times; and (3) a reconstruction of our contemporary experience according to the light both of man's reason and of a divinely revealed Faith. The value of the thought of Marcel is that his philosophy incorporates at least some of the elements of this type of existentialism.

Perhaps one of the most significant things a person can say of the thought of Marcel is that it represents a highly personalized quest for wisdom. Marcel is not the initiator of a school of philosophy or, least of all, of any kind of system: his thinking rather is in the tradition of Socrates, Augustine, Pascal, and Kierkegaard, the tradition of men who encountered truth the "hard way" along the thorny path of conflict and struggle, not only against the powers of evil, regarded as something outside the person himself, but against the devil that lies within. To Marcel the greatest enemy of personal development is not mass society which organizes itself against man, but the fundamental selfishness that is latent in every member of the race. Accordingly, some of the fundamental themes of his philosophy are the need for man to escape the limitations of his own existence, the status of man as a wayfarer, the necessity for a kind of philosophy that is open to mystical insight, and the need for identifying our purposes as individuals, both with one another and with the yet higher purpose that God has in mind for the universe at large. In the balance of this essay I can no more than touch upon some of these themes.

Let me proceed with Marcel's notion of philosophy: for him philosophy is not a *fait accompli*, a neat set of propositions that would provide one with a sure guide for living. Rather, the fundamental condition of the philosopher, as for mankind in general, is that of *homo viator*, of man as wayfarer. Better yet, philosophy is a way of intuiting life from the point of view of *homo viator*, of a man who is always "on the road," always traveling, and has not yet arrived and will not arrive until the very moment of his death. Marcel's approach to philosophy is, therefore, something to "get with," not to "arrive at." Indeed, it has been pointed out by one of the authorities on Marcel that this fundamentally elusive character of his work is a built-in feature of the work itself, one of its essential characteristics.[2] Philosophy, for him as it was earlier for William James, is always a tentative statement of truth, of the truth of personal living, subject to revision and subject to new insights and new truths. Though in a different sense perhaps than James, Marcel is a "radical empiricist," or, as he characterizes himself, a neo-socratic, and the fundamental work of a socratic

---

[2] Cf. K. T. Gallagher, *The Philosophy of Gabriel Marcel* (New York: Fordham University Press, 1952), p. 2 ff.

is more to raise fundamental questions than to have a ready supply of dogmatic answers.

Given this basically socratic orientation of Marcel's philosophy, it is a matter of no surprise that his approach to metaphysics is not the impersonal, objective one of a detached observer, but rather one of *humility before being* and personal involvement. Such an attitude implies a recognition of a depth in being which surpasses and includes us. Man, in other words, is himself too highly immersed in the mystery of being to make any overall statements of its character as though he could completely transcend it. On this point, there seems to be a very close resemblance between the thought of Marcel and that of Bergson, another "philosopher of the concrete." For Marcel, as for Bergson earlier, it is a tragic mistake for philosophers to imagine that they can enclose being within the narrow framework of their own paltry efforts at conceptualization. Because of its mysterious character, being is something that can easily elude us, especially if we try to capture it with a net. On this last point, not only philosophers, but scientists too, fail to know reality as it is, whenever they contract it, so to speak, to the dimensions of their own specialized approach to reality.

Concerning the situation of man-in-the-world, Marcel is insistent on the fact that man is not his soul. Moreover, it is a mistaken point of view to imagine that the body (my body) is only an appendage to my being, and in this respect, although Marcel refers to himself as a neo-socratic, he is certainly not a neo-platonist. To the contrary, in Marcel's view every man *is* his body in the sense that the body is the concrete, material manifestation of the person himself. Moreover, and this thought is basic to the "personalism" of Marcel, one never exists in isolation from others but only in interpersonal communion with his fellowmen. This is a dominant theme of his work as it was a dominant theme of the philosophy of Josiah Royce by whom Marcel was influenced, and as it is a theme also of the work of Father Teilhard. In a word, man grows and lives by a vital and interpersonal union with and through his fellowman. Isolation can only lead to stagnation.

To the extent that Marcel insists throughout his work on man's need for loving his fellowman (in contrast, let us say, to Sartre's rigid insistence on a certain type of selfish freedom), it can be said that Marcel's metaphysics is not only a metaphysics of being, but of love, of a love that involves a being-present to one's fellowman:

> In this world of things presence is apt to lose its character or its proper value or to be reduced to a simple being-there — "*Dasein.*" But it is in the higher realm of relationship with other persons that presence may and must re-appear, and this chiefly on account of what can be designated by the general word "encounter."

> Here is a very simple example to make myself understood. Let us think, if you like, of a conductor whom we have habitually to deal with in the daily train or bus ride to our work — to our office. At the start, this man has for us only the functional reality bounded with the fact of punching tickets or of driving the vehicle. But let us imagine that something unusual draws our attention to him. For instance, a sign of physical suffering, or perhaps of some moral distress. The link between us ceases to be purely functional. This man becomes really a human being for us — a *presence!* And this will perhaps extend itself through the question which I shall perhaps ask him, if I succeed in mastering my discretion or my natural shyness.

> Let us suppose in questioning I ask him, "What is the matter?" And he answers me, perhaps moved to see that he has aroused my interest. In this way we become really present to one another, at least for a brief moment. It is the dawn of what I call inter-subjectivity, that is to say, mutual openness. . . .

> From this moment we become presentially aware of one another. . . . We are on the verge of becoming interior to one another. But, of course, this interiority is only fully

realized, that is to say, effected in love or more precisely in true *Agape*.[3]

In light of Marcel's insistence on love, openness to others, intersubjectivity, and so on, it should be clear that our basic ontological posture should be that of a kind of availability to our fellowman. We fully become ourselves when we place ourselves, not as instruments, but as persons, at the disposition of those whom we serve.

Happily then, the starting point of metaphysics for Marcel is not, as it was for Descartes, "I think," but "we are"; and it is this need for authentic togetherness and personal communion that comprises one of the most relevant themes of his work. This theme is relevant to the problem of rescuing contemporary man from the impersonal forces of a technology that tends to get out of hand and to reduce him to the level of mere function. As Marcel insists, we too often identify a man in terms of what he does rather than what he is, e.g., as a policeman who blows his whistle to keep traffic in line, or as a nurse who administers an anesthetic to prepare a patient for an operation. Here the real necessity is that of transcending not only one's own petty egotism but the forces of a technology that tend to depersonalize man. What is needed is for man to learn how to live with his fellowman in a way that is properly human.

Intimately connected with this line of thought is Marcel's distinction between "problem" and "mystery." The meaning of the distinction may readily be grasped by the fact that problematic knowledge is knowledge of the object *as object*, that is, as something that is external to myself who regards the object from the mere point of view of a *spectator*. Knowledge of a mystery, by contrast, is knowledge in which I become personally involved *as a subject*. In the best and most literal sense of the term such knowledge is *subjective*. The "object" of this kind of cognition is something I ap-

---

[3] From an address which Marcel delivered at De Paul University, Chicago, Fall of 1963.

proach with respect, and for the purpose, not of de-flowering its intelligibility, but of becoming absorbed into it and becoming transformed by it. A mystery of whatever sort, natural (like the mystery of my own being) or supernatural (like the mystery of divine grace freely given to man by God), is something that encompasses *me* and not I, *it*.

No doubt this last aspect of Marcel's thought leads to many fruitful consequences insofar as it points up the need for what I should like to call "the realm of true subjectivity." The realm of true subjectivity is not a realm that each person must *create* for himself as though it were no more than a product of his own feverish imagination. Rather it is a realm which a person — if he is patient enough to pursue it — will *discover* for himself; it is a realm of mystery, the mystery that lies within one's being, such as the mystery of the presence of God within the human soul. To plunge, then, into the realm of true subjectivity is not to invent a means of escape or retreat from the "real" world, but to exercise the highest form of courage. It takes great courage aggressively to uncover the most hidden recesses of our being so as to discover our own real and authentic selves.

This being so, I would wager that the real escapists are those who retreat into an exclusive realm of outer events, who confront a world of objects as objects, in the hope of "losing themselves" and in the hope of avoiding those problems within themselves that must be faced if life for them is to have any real meaning, and this is one of the great mistakes of our times: to think that the inner world of human experience has no meaning or existence because we have no scientific means of coping with it, of measuring it, or of domesticating it to our own utilitarian ends or purposes.

It is no exaggeration, in view of all this, to say that Marcel is an enemy of any attempt to regard everything from the impersonal point of view of an object that can be handled or of a problem that can be solved. Most important of all, one's fellowman is not simply an object that exists alongside other objects to be treated as though he were a tool: rather he is there to be loved, to be administered to, and, if need be, to be reproached, corrected, or put into jail.[4]

To conclude, I want to say that the basic virtues Marcel emphasizes are those of fidelity, love, and hope. Since the philosophy of Marcel has sometimes been called a *metaphysics of hope*, it may be well to reflect here that the efficacy of hope lies in its foreswearing of egotistic armament. To hope is not to thrust oneself forward, but to retire absolutely in favor of an absolute. Hope has no weapons, it knows no techniques.[5] Such, then, is the perspective of a Christian philosopher who counters atheistic despair with a deep-seated commitment to hope, who in the face of contemporary man's defiance both of God's laws and those of his own nature emphasizes the need for fidelity and obedience, and who, finally, in the place of an impersonal approach to man and society advocates the growing need for a love and unity that pervades the whole of mankind. Understood in this, its highest dimension, "existentialism" is a philosophy that is admirably suited to the needs of our times.

* * *

See also Topic Six, No. 1;
Topic Twelve, No. 6;
Topic Fourteen, No. 1;
Topic Sixteen, No. 8.

---

[4] Though Emerson can hardly be classified as an existentialist, compare Emerson's protest against mass society in the nineteenth century with the protest of Marcel and others in the twentieth. Thus: "The state of society is one in which the members have suffered amputation from the trunk, and strut about so many walking monsters. . . . The planter, who is Man sent out into the field to gather food is seldom cheered by any idea of the true dignity of his ministry. He sees his bushel and his cart, and nothing beyond, and sinks into the farmer, instead of Man on the farm. The tradesman scarcely ever gives an ideal worth to his work, but is ridden by the routine of his craft, and the soul is subject to dollars. The priest becomes a form; the attorney a statute-book; the mechanic a machine; the sailor a rope of the ship." R. Emerson, "The American Scholar," as quoted from Mueldner-Sears-Schlabach, *The Development of American Philosophy* (Boston: Houghton Mifflin Co., 1960), p. 148.

[5] *The Philosophy of Gabriel Marcel*, p. 74.

CHAPTER ELEVEN

A CONVENTION TRIP TO NEW YORK
AND THE SPIRIT OF AMERICAN
NATURALISM

Over the years I have had occasion to attend a variety of philosophical conventions but none of them quite so reward- ing as the one I attended in New York in the winter of 1962. I had been asked much earlier to deliver a commentary on a paper that would be given by Professor James K. Feibleman under the title "Knowing, Doing, and Being." Presently I shall say more of this paper, but first a word on certain as- pects of the trip itself.

It was the second day after Christmas that I made the trip to New York, and once there I had occasion to see Bolt's now famous play on the life of Thomas More, *A Man for All Seasons*. The play was most enjoyable, but even more so was the pleasure of making the acquaintance of a British naval officer who sat next to me during the play, and who had previously seen the play in London. In a conversation we had after the performance my friend frankly admitted that he was a "kind of agnostic" — but that he had a pro- found admiration for St. Thomas More. As he put it, what he admired was the "moral fiber of the man." Regretting as he did the breakdown of morals in society, he wondered in his own mind about such questions as to the ultimate meaning of life which we discussed to a very late hour. Yet the time arrived to go back to the hotel for a night's sleep that was altogether too brief.

Dr. Feibleman's talk was a remarkably capable affair and worthy of his reputation for urbanity. The subject of the talk revolved on the question of human needs, and the basic thesis of the author was the naturalistic one — that all human needs are ultimately traceable to a purely biological source. In the course of his talk he spoke of man's fundamental need for knowing, doing, and being. Against the background of these topics I now provide for the reader the following excerpts from my own commentary on Dr. Feibleman's talk. These comments will help the reader to see for himself some crucial points of difference between a realistic naturalism (such as Feibleman's) and a realistic thomism (such as my own).

"As the Italians say, *molto bisogno che* — 'there is much need' — and at this moment I feel 'compelled' to reduce my need to offer some few comments on Feibleman's talk. Barring the question as to the source of his need and mine to philosophize, I hereby acknowledge my debt to the speaker for using a language that has a manner and a style of expression not too greatly different in clarity from the articles he writes for the *Saturday Review*."

At this point I delved into some of the more technical aspects of Feibleman's paper, particularly his distinction between "primary" and "secondary" needs. Significantly, "primary" needs were for him the basic biological ones, and "secondary" meant the whole gamut of man's social, cultural, moral needs.

The commentary continues as follows:

"Concerning the existence of primary needs, which is to say man's need for *water*, *food*, and *sex*, we can only agree with the author. Yet the question I would raise is whether all of man's secondary needs *so-called* (like his need for a beneficent love of his fellows) are in any sense reducible to his need for a drink, a meal, or a mate? Is it not possible, in other words, that some of these 'secondary' needs may not themselves be primary in consideration of the nature of man as such, especially the higher side of his nature?[1] I am not questioning, of course, the fact that every need has some kind of a biological base, but I do question whether the biological base of human behavior is the ultimate source of its origin as well as the ultimate point of its return."

As I review this part of my commentary, I can only think of the need, the very real need, of my friend of the preceding evening to discover the meaning of life. Surely this need was no projection of his creative imagination, nor was his hunger for the answer to life's problems to be confused with his hunger for the material comforts of life. This British naval officer has, I am sure, certain specialized needs of his own, but the basic need for meaning, ultimate meaning, is as primary as any might be. But let me continue my commentary:

"I fear that the speaker's treatment of so-called secondary needs has been too severely naturalistic both in tone and in content to do full justice to the facts, nor can I possibly agree with him when he says that human behavior like animal behavior can be accounted for by the search to reduce the drives. Surely the speaker himself would be the last to confuse the need for writing books or composing music with the need, let us say, for toilet training or eating Wheaties. Yet there is doubt in this person's mind whether 'the search to reduce the drives' provides a satisfactory basis on theoretical grounds for the origin of such different types of needs from the lowest level 'primary' ones to our highest level 'secondary' needs. I am not, of course, idealizing man's secondary needs and there is no fear in my mind that Dr.

---

[1] For an example, a good measure of human activity is employed, if you will, in the reduction of the needs of my neighbor. Often too this results in a consequent increase in my own as when I give the last dollar I own to a friend. The point is that a man often acts out of the highest motives of love with little or no concern for the consequences that he himself must bear.

Feibleman would, but I should like to think that both he and I as philosophers are obliged to concern ourselves with the *source* of the differences wherever the differences exist. To apply to them what would appear as a preconceived theory of animalistic drives is, in this critic's view, a rather filtered method for the admission of evidence which in its pure form might be damaging to the theory.

"Let us consider, for example, man's 'response' to the need *to be* after death. Granting that death itself is not a myth, why on Dr. Feibleman's hypothesis should man plague himself with the 'myth' of a soul that survives *post mortem?* Or must it be assumed a *priori* that this — like all of man's other 'secondary' needs — is no more than the result of a psychosomatic drive that finds its roots in the blind unconscious of the ego? Further, barring such a preconception as this, is it not possible that man's belief in survival may be based on the ontological situation of man himself insofar as he can and does transcend in *some* of his operations the limitations of his natural environment. And if such be the case, then the whole question of needs — especially man's need for religion — would have to be reexamined in a far more *objective* light than it does in the naturalistic psychologism of the author. In short, I suspect that the theory of need reduction as a behavioral affair bears in its present form a heavier load of values than it can credibly sustain.

"I, therefore, leave the audience with this question: what do our needs need in order for them to make sense from the point of view of their objective referents — where it is openly judged to be possible that such referents actually do exist? The answer to this question may not be easy to probe, but it is one that philosophers as the potentially wise men of some future age can hardly choose to minimize, deface, or ignore."

Post Scriptum: Having delivered my commentary and having listened to Dr. Feibleman's capable response, I served him a glass of water to reduce one of his primary needs *and my own*. The convention so far as I was personally concerned, ended on this happy note, but with the thought in mind that in a pluralistic society such as our own it is necessary for philosophers to confront each other with their differences. Lacking such confrontation, it is doubtful that any solid progress can be made toward the acquisition of truth. The return home by jet was smooth: *per aspera ad astra*.

*   *   *

See also Topic Four, Nos. 1–6;
Topic Fifteen, No. 15;
Topic Nineteen, No. 1.

CHAPTER TWELVE

THOUGHTS ON FATHER TEILHARD

In recent years a vast new sun has begun to shine on the horizons of Christian thought in the person and writings of Father Teilhard de Chardin. The purpose of this essay is not to give an account of the scientific work of Father Teilhard, as that is outside the scope of my inquiry. Rather I want to convey to the reader something of the "magnificence" of the man and his work, and I use that term in the sense in which St. Thomas habitually speaks of it as a virtue which lies in a certain greatness of soul, of a willingness, even a passionate desire, to embark upon some great work or synthesis.

Amid countless travels it was Teilhard's lifework to provide the beginnings of a new synthesis of Christian thought. He himself was a scientist who spent the better part of his life collecting fossils, testing rock formations with his hammer, and giving papers when necessary to scientific groups and conventions. As a scientist his work lay in the field of palaeontology, which has to do with the study of the past. Yet neither the closeness of this man to the earth nor his professional preoccupation with the past prevented him from becoming both a mystic and a great humanitarian whose consuming desire was to see all men unite in a common effort at "building up the universe" for the glory of God.

Repeatedly he emphasizes this point in his writing, namely, that the past as such holds no interest for him as his central concern is to develop an "overview" that looks to what man will do with his past toward the future of the race. The basically Christian perspective of the work of Teilhard is profoundly influenced by the deep-seated conviction that — in a radically Pauline sense — the world is God's world through the Redemption of the Risen Christ. It is the Risen Christ who is the hidden Ruler of everything in the universe from the most seemingly insignificant form of life to that remarkable piece of creation that is man.

The vocabulary of Teilhard is strange at times, as when he commonly links such terms as cosmogenesis, biogenesis, noögensis, homogenesis, Christogenesis, and the like. Too, there is much in his writings that is ambiguous, such as the view that all matter is incipiently conscious, yet no one who reads Teilhard can miss his total dedication to the fundamentally evolutionary character of the universe. To him the movement of the universe is an upward movement of evolution that seeks an ever greater unity of things and events through a process that he calls "convergence." Whatever its scientific details, the important thing to note concerning the *Christian* evolutionism of Teilhard is the basic principle that *the lower exists for the higher* and seeks the higher principle for its fulfillment and perfection.

In one sense this principle is as old as Christian thought itself, and it was one of the dominant keynotes of Aquinas. What is remarkable about Teilhard, however, is that he gives this principle a whole new setting and focus in a way that seeks an ever greater integration between Christian thought and the world of twentieth-century science. So far no other thinker has ever so thoroughly incorporated within an evolutionary view of the universe the principle of spiritual evolution that involves a principle of absolute transcendence over the inherent limitations of matter.

As it is not my intent, however, to go into the details of Teilhard's scientific thought, I want to pass on now to two events that have made a profound impact on my own personal estimation of the man. The first event was my chancing upon *The Divine Milieu* during a retreat at the Trappist Monastery in Ava, Missouri, and the second was my receiving his *Letters from a Traveller* as a Christmas gift from my wife. It was the reading of both of these books (the one "spiritual," the other a sort of autobiography) that conveyed to me the flesh and blood character of the man. The perspective of *The Divine Milieu* is sketched by the author in his introduction to the work as follows:

> To some, the world has disclosed itself as too vast: with such immensity, man is lost and no longer counts; and there is nothing for him to do but shut his eyes and disappear. To others, the world is too beautiful; and it, and it alone, must be adored.

> There are Christians, as there are men, who remain unaffected by these feelings of anxiety or fascination. The following pages are not for them. But there are others who are alarmed by the agitation or the attraction invisibly produced in them by this new rising star. . . . Is the world not in the process of becoming more vast, more close, more dazzling than Jehovah? Will it not burst our religion asunder? Eclipse our God?

> I shall not attempt to embark on metaphysics or apologetics. Instead, I shall turn back, with those who care to follow me to the Agora. There, in each other's company we shall listen to St. Paul telling the Areopagites of "God, who made man that he might seek Him. . . ." . . . This little book does no more than recapitulate the eternal lesson of the Church in the words of a man who, *because he believes himself to feel deeply in tune with his own times,* has sought to teach *how to see God everywhere,* to see Him in all that is most hidden, most solid and most ultimate in the world. . . . Without immixture, without confusion, the true God, the Christian God, will, under your gaze, invade the universe, our universe of today, the universe which so frightened you by its alarming size or its pagan beauty. . . . He will become for you universally tangible and active — very near and very distant at one and the same time.[1]

---

[1] Pierre Teilhard de Chardin, *The Divine Milieu*, trans. by B. Wall (New York: Harper & Row, Publ., 1960), pp. 13–15. (Italics my own.)

What finer introduction to a work whose basic intent is to lead one's contemporaries back to God? The whole of *The Divine Milieu* is a sort of spiritual odyssey that provides a profound measure of strength and comfort to contemporary man in the midst of his journey through life. It is a concrete attempt to reinstate Christ in the universe of the twentieth century.

On a yet more personal level I should like now, however, to pass to Teilhard's *Letters* and the inspiration they provided me with while I read them during a Christmas holiday in Dallas. Here I can do no better than to quote from my own book of notes jotted down at the time I read this fascinating book.

*　　*　　*

Notes, dated Sunday, December 29, 1963, on *Letters from a Traveller*

I feel completely *sympatico* with this marvelous person who incorporates the qualities both of a scientific genius and a saint. His life: b. May 1, 1881, d. April 10 (Easter Sunday in New York), 1955. But so much happened in between. Learned natural history from his father; gathered specimens early in life; liked iron; enjoyed using his hammer to test rock formations.

Outstanding Features of the Man. His insatiable curiosity to know, at first (as he traveled through the Suez) places and things, and later to know people (but this, as he said, would come later). Felt deeply within himself the sacral character of the universe, the "transparency" of matter, the Presence of the God-Man as the Ruler of All, as the cosmic yet deeply and immensely personal Christ. Had a warm, sensitive heart; felt at home in the world of electrons, neutrons, protons, and molecules. Salvation is to be found, not in the abandonment of the world, but by participation in it. At 42, as he left Marseilles for Tientsin, he felt as though he had reached the limits of his powers. As he put it, he was unable to keep things in mind and he thought he was going to die:

The only way out was to cling to a blind and absolute faith that God is the animating source of every event (in our lives), even of our diminishments.[2]

After a number of years of travel and scientific exploration, Teilhard made this remarkable statement in a letter to a friend:

I am convinced that the only true science we can acquire in this ocean of weakness and ignorance is the vision that begins to take shape under the multiplicity of things.[3]

It was the pursuit of this *vision* that seemed to be his chief preoccupation through the whole of his life.

Personal Comment. The calling of every Christian, I take it to be, is to look for a principle of mystical unity that threads all the disparate events of our life into a central purpose. There is so much that is scattered and seemingly disparate, and when the principle of unity does appear, it seems to tantalize us for but a fleeting moment. Underneath it all, however, this principle of unity is there as surely as we tread the face of the earth, doing what we think and know to be God's will. Our great trial is that *we can do no more than catch an occasional glimpse of the unity and drama of life,* but no need here for great concern or anxiety. It is the "fate" of us all to be under the burden of *time* and the uncertain movement that it implies. What is now so scattered and disparate will be bound together when the day of eternity dawns, and there is no need for fear, provided that we do each day the work that lies in store and as the very circumstances of our lives prescribe. We are serving God if we serve the events *and persons* He places in our lives, and the magnitude or comparative insignificance of the task should be no concern of ours. The motto of the Christian, as of every man, should be to serve God in the place in which He

[2] Pierre Teilhard de Chardin, *Letters from a Traveller*, trans. by B. Wall (New York: Harper & Row, Publ., 1962), p. 28.

[3] *Ibid.*, p. 86.

is found. As someone once put it, *God wants you where you are needed.*

Father Teilhard on Travel. In a letter written from Tientsin to a friend and dated October 15, 1923, Father Teilhard makes this interesting statement as a reflection on a journey he had made:

> The journey was over, and I felt keenly how little, of itself, mere displacement in space adds to a man. On returning to his point of departure, unless he has developed his inner life — a thing which doesn't show outwardly — he is still exactly like everyone else.[4]

Personal Comment. In the above quotation Teilhard's commitment to the principle of interior growth is made quite explicit. Yet the problem is this. How can or should one separate or distill his interior life of prayer from all the distractions of life? No doubt, Teilhard would answer that in a sense our life *is* the very distractions that make it up, and the point of a true interior life (for those few of us who possess it securely) is to unify these distractions into a principle of spiritual unity with the realization that the distractions themselves are the very matter, the very content of our life. Consequently, we make a mistake to pursue the "spiritual" all by itself and in a sort of autonomous vacuum. If we do, then the spiritual becomes static, it dries up, and we too. And so, for a man in the world neither a purely spiritual life nor a life of multitudinous distractions is the answer to happiness. What is needed is that the distractions become synthesized and incorporated into a higher principle which is a mystical one, and dependent alike upon our own efforts, but for the most part on God's grace. To paraphrase Teilhard, the only true science is mysticism because it unifies and synthesizes what is scattered and discrete.

Teilhard on Complete Dedication. As one reads the works of Teilhard, one has a profound awareness of a man who is completely dedicated to his mission in life — a mission that

---

[4] *Ibid.,* p. 91.

is not always clear and often requires an "openness to the light" that few souls seem to possess. In any case, the perspective of the man is that of an authentic openness to the whole of things, or to things taken in their totality. Thus:

> Individual events [I take it in their pure state of isolation] count for nothing . . . all that really matters is devotion to something bigger than ourselves.[5]

Surely the great trap that every man is exposed to in varying degrees is that of preoccupation with oneself — a trap that leads to the door of utter madness and confusion. The only way to avoid this trap and to project oneself outside of the ego is this "devotion to something bigger than ourselves." In another context Teilhard expresses the same basic thought:

> To hold fast to only one thing . . . a really precise, concrete thing, so exalted and so great that it sheds its light on everything else — here lies the summit of happiness.[6]

Is not this quotation a poignant reminder of the title of one of Kierkegaard's books which affirms the truth that "To love God is to will one thing." But how is this to be taken? Surely, not in the sense of the meaningless repetition of one and the same kind of act, as life itself is characterized by an immense variety of things? It should be taken rather in the sense that whatever the variety, all things — however diverse — must be sought after under the same basic "formal object" which is the love of God. It is this principle that establishes not a monotonous sameness, but a radical continuity in our lives.

On the One-and-the-Many and Insight Into the Real World. In one of his letters Teilhard is mildly critical of what he regards as a defect in his past education. In his view the approach to the problem of the one-and-the-many has been *overly metaphysical,* and I personally delight in the way in which he expresses this point:

---

[5] *Ibid.,* p. 104.
[6] *Ibid.*

I find that the single great problem of the One and the Manifold is rapidly beginning to emerge from the overlay-metaphysical context in which I used to state it and look for its solution. I can now see more clearly that its urgency and its difficulties must be in terms of real men and women. [From a letter dated April 15, 1913.][7]

In this remarkable quotation Teilhard is not casting out the light of metaphysics, but only insisting on the need for focusing its problems on the real world, especially the world as it affects our lives in terms of the men and women who make it up. What Teilhard seems to be rejecting is a too highly academic, rationalistic, and idealistic approach to the problems of metaphysics, and I personally could not be in fuller agreement with the man. Here I can only reiterate the wisdom of teaching metaphysics in our schools, but along with it the need for building metaphysics on the basis of an authentic human experience. A too highly rigid, too formalized approach to metaphysics can only lead to a certain type of stagnation. Moreover, the natural wisdom that is philosophy must remain open to a yet higher light which is the light of Faith and to the still higher light of a mystical unity that transcends, not Faith, but all ordinary experience.

On one of his travels Teilhard had occasion to witness a beautiful sunset reflecting its manifold light in a setting of water and cliff. Speaking of this, he makes this astute remark:

Professors of theology [and I suppose he would include professors of philosophy too] would do well to have a spell of what I am doing now. I am beginning to think that there is a certain aspect of the real world as closed to some believers as the world of faith is to unbelievers.[8]

A tremendously powerful thought here which suggests the idea that no man can live by books alone! To know reality truly one must be open to new sources of light and refreshment; one must, as it were, come up for air and regain his

7 *Ibid.*, pp. 66–67.
8 *Ibid.*, p. 66.

perspective whether it be through the medium of social intercourse, proximity to nature, or some kind of manual work. Excessive preoccupation with books can lead to a one-sided development of a man whatever his learning and brilliance.[9] As Teilhard expresses himself elsewhere: "In isolation a man stops either thinking or advancing."[10] We are told by one of the cousins of Teilhard, Mlle. Teilhard-Chambon, that he had the sort of mind that needs to retain and even multiply its contacts with the world outside; if he was to give substance to his thought or precision to his own personal ideas, he had to discuss his way of seeing things with other people.

Conclusion. Having thus quoted from my diary account of reflections on the *Travels* of Teilhard, I find it difficult to sum up in a few words what actually are the most remarkable features of this great thinker of our times. To some persons it is his indomitable optimism, to others his faith both in God and mankind. It is worth noting, however, that Teilhard had a great love of life and, as I have previously remarked, an insatiable curiosity to know. We are told:

> . . . The one fault he detested, the one he would have nothing to do with, was the deliberate acceptance and delight in disgust with life, contempt for the works of man, fear of the human effort. For Pere Teilhard this lack of confidence in the efficacy of man's vocation was the real sin. Our natural weaknesses could be looked upon with indulgence so long as the desire to rise, to progress . . . was sincere. . . . In pushing human aspirations to the most daring extreme, man may ascend to the heights. It was this he had in mind when he used to say "We must dare all things."[11]

---

[9] Note the same thought as it is expressed by Emerson: "Instead of Man Thinking, we have the bookworm. Hence the book-learned class, who value books as such. . . . Hence the bibliomaniacs of all degrees. Books are the best of things, well used; abused, among the worst. . . . They are for nothing but to inspire." R. W. Emerson, "The American Scholar," reproduced in Mueldner-Sears-Schlabach, *The Development of American Philosophy* (Boston: Houghton, Mifflin, 1960), p. 149.

[10] *Letters for a Traveller*, p. 74.

[11] *Letters*, from an Introduction by Pierre Leroy, S.J., p. 46.

Finally, it must be emphasized that the fundamental motivation of his thought was profoundly religious, profoundly Christian. That he was no mere Christian pietist may be gathered from the following quote:

> The more I look into myself the more I find myself possessed by the conviction that it is only the science of Christ *running through all things*, that is the true mystical science, that really matters.[12]

Herein, then, lies the measure of the greatness of the man, namely, his unique ability to integrate in his personal life his Christian commitment with his commitment to the values of the world. Christian perfection is not a goal to be pursued in independence from the world, as it is the world itself that needs through all the variant forms of human activity to be consecrated to God. It was the leadership Teilhard has provided in pointing upward to the path of this consecration that makes him the figure of such importance that he is.

*   *   *

See also Topic Four, No. 6;
Topic Nine, Nos. 4–5;
Topic Fourteen, No. 5.

---

[12] *Ibid.*, pp. 85–86.

CHAPTER THIRTEEN

VALUES IN AMERICA

The title of this essay might easily include material for an entire book; as a matter of fact, it was inspired precisely by a book of that name, *Values in America*, published by the Notre Dame University Press in 1961. It is not so much my intent, however, to give a résumé of this book as it is to touch upon a number of topics that have important implications for life in America as we know it today.

The first question I would raise concerns the much-vaunted "American way of life," and whether or not this "way of life" as many persons understand it is worth preserving. But let us begin with the meaning and use of the term "Americanism." By "Americanism" some people mean a certain habit of mind, an attitude that involves on their part a total commitment, a sort of religious devotion to the American way of life. The chief values of this way of life are freedom, individual enterprise, an attitude of suspicion in regard to other nations, and a certain brand of patriotism that rather closely identifies itself with all the appearances of the virtue of patriotism, its external trappings, such as flag-waving and button-wearing, but seldom with the real thing. "Americanism" to these persons is a kind of nationalism which combines national pride with a tradition of condescending tolerance or even hostility toward other nations or persons who are not part of the group mentality I have just attempted to describe.

Concerning this brand of "Americanism" little need be said except to remark that it is a distortion of the best tradition of American thought and American life. Few persons, for an example, will agree that the era of the McCarthy investigations in the 1950's was one of which this nation might be justly proud. During this period there was, of course, the threat of the enemy — namely, Communist infiltration of some government agencies — that many persons minimized or chose to ignore. Yet the manner in which this threat was countered by a militant right-wing group represented an approach to the problem that was in many respects worse than the evil it was intended to cure. This era was one of open suspicion of one's fellow citizens on the grounds that they *might be* members of the enemy ranks; it was an era in which everyone had to *prove* — whether by loyalty oaths or other tests — that he was a "100 percent American." "Americanism" in this sense of the word is a form of extremism, and it is likely that there will always be extremists — to the left and to the right — on the American scene. Happily, however, the best tradition of American life has not been one of political extremes, and this brings me back to the question of values in American political life. What are the basic values to which most Americans subscribe and why do they hold them?

Fundamentally, the "American way of life" in its best sense stands for a set of values that are in radical opposition to any form of totalitarian government that would stamp out the rights of the individual. These values are epitomized (1) in the conviction that every individual is a person who possesses an inherent dignity of his own, and (2) in the desire to share the burdens of other citizens and other nations whenever it is possible to do so. By contrast, a totalitarian regime in its very essence represents a kind of thinking, "philosophical" if we may call it such, which maintains that the worth of the individual is to be judged only in terms of his usefulness to the state. Under such a system the inherent value of the person — together with his inviolable rights — is obscured, sometimes swallowed up, in the all-encompassing arms of a quasi-omnipotent state.

The question as to why Americans maintain the values they do is not an easy one to answer, as very few of them are reflective enough to make explicit for themselves a philosophy of certain truths which they hold dear. Even so, with or without a philosophy there is a basic moderateness of judgment, a deposit of good sense that sustains the American people in difficult periods of crisis, even when they are plagued in their own society by extremists.

Lest it be thought, however, that the presence of extremists is the only factor that gives rise to the problems of American life one should recall that the basic tension in a democracy such as this is the tension between freedom and order. In fact, the whole mechanism of American government is a sort of compromise between the principle of order and efficiency, on the one hand, and the principle of democratic freedom on the other. It is true that the tradition of American democracy — again in its best sense — is a tradition of reason, but not without some sort of qualification. In one sense it is "unreasonable" and highly contrary to a *perfectly ordered society* (if such a society exists) that so much time and effort should be expended in the business of electing officials from the level of alderman all the way up to the President of the United States. Many a foreigner might have cause to wonder why there should be so many political campaigns. He might also wonder how it is possible — out of the pandemonium of national political conventions — to elect a responsible leader who will direct the policies of an entire nation for a minimum of four years in the highest office in the land.

Yet, however unreasonable this cumbersome procedure might otherwise seem to be, the system itself, in spite of its defects, is one that has stood the test both of time (however limited) and experience. Concerning the "rationality" of this way of government one should plainly acknowledge that American democracy is no more a *purely* rational system than

is man himself *purely* rational.[1] Yet it is rational enough to
allow minority groups — however extremist they may be —
to have their say-so provided they be kept under control. The
genius of American politics, so it seems, is to maintain this
difficult sense of balance (as though in a tightrope act) between law and order on the one hand and a large amount of
political and other kinds of confusion on the other. The
fundamental paradox, then, is that of a system which works
in spite of itself because of a commitment to order that
does not go beyond the minimum requirements of a society
that is free and capable of making decisions for itself.

Since this essay is concerned with the question of values
it should be asserted, therefore, that the values of the American commitment to both order and freedom have been
proven to be basically sound, but not on that account im-
mune from constant self-examination. The American system
as we know it has worked so far, but do we have a guarantee
that it will continue to work in the future, and in any case
is there or should there be such a thing as a political philosophy for the nation as a whole?

Let me address myself to this last question. If by a "philosophy" one means here a political ideology, then I would
say the answer should be "no." An ideology, as I understand
it, is a prescribed set of doctrines that is superimposed from
above (and that in an arbitrary manner) on the mass of
the people as a whole. Little or no appeal here is made to
the people's intelligence, and the people themselves are regarded only as the instruments of a government which usually
is in fact if not in name *dictatorial*. Too, ideology thrives
on propaganda, and it is hardly consistent for a democracy to
maintain itself by means of propaganda — as though the
people at large cannot somehow judge for themselves. For
this and other reasons a "philosophy" of government in the

---

[1] Even in Plato one finds the comparison between the lower elements or
"passions" within man the individual and within the state at large, and the
need for subjugating these lower elements to the higher.

sense of an ideology is completely undesirable and unwise.

This is not to say, however, that no kind of philosophy should prevail within a democracy. If it is true to say in individual cases that the unexamined life is unworthy of man, then is it not true for all the more reason of a nation as a whole? Why, in other words, should anyone imagine that it is good for individual persons to have a philosophy of life or of government and not good for the nation as a whole? At this point, however, we touch on a very important question: whether beyond the minimum requirements of the American Constitution itself there should be such a thing as a philosophy that motivates American society at large.

As an answer to this question it would seem that there is such a thing as a *hidden* philosophy involved in the American way of life, and *because* it is hidden difficult to analyze, difficult, as it were, to "pin down." Thus it is generally admitted that however vague the goals of the American way of life, it is false to assume from this that the American way of life — taken in its best sense as an enterprise that works for the good of humanity — has *no* ideals or goals. As one author puts it "America believes in and aspires to something much higher than its plane of actual life."

Now the problem that arises is this: whether it is good or desirable to take this "hidden" philosophy and make it far more explicit than it actually is and, if so, how? Although some authors argue that it is best to keep our philosophy hidden,[2] the danger of this approach is, I think, that it commits one to a permanent state of confusion. I entirely agree, for an example, with the basic motivation of President Eisenhower who during his years of office assembled a group of men for the precise purpose of examining our national purpose. Although the results of this particular effort may have had no more than a limited success, the basic attempt was, I think, not only well motivated, but sound.

---

[2] See for an example David Boorstin, *The Genius of American Politics* (Chicago: University of Chicago Press, 1959).

As to the method of developing a far more explicit philosophy of values in American life it would be a mistake, I am sure, to leave this to the work of politicians alone. More especially the business of defining values is a work that should come from the "bottom up rather than from the top down." This means, in effect, that various organizations within our American society should commit themselves to a far more thorough examination of their particular goals in relation to the overall goals of American society at large. In particular, the work of American education should include as no small part of its overall endeavor a reexamination of the bases of American political and sociocultural life. On the question of values, American society is divided in theory (and partly also in practice) between a positivistic, secularistic approach to our national traditions and one that stresses the bases of these traditions in terms of the natural law. It is these very issues that should be examined and discussed in a fair-minded way in all of our American universities, private and public alike, and that without prejudice to the fact that there is a fundamental division of opinion on this score. In any event, it is a mistake to ignore the question of values as though the whole effort of American education should be restricted to the mere communication of skills. On this point a truly liberal education is one that *transcends* the mere communication of skills and embraces the *wider realm of ideas* and the *manner* in which those ideas are relevant to the actual cultural conditions of the society in which we live.

As an example of the *kind* of self-criticism that should be carried on in our schools I submit the following quote from Senator Eugene McCarthy:

Let us look at the general level of morality in the United States. It is a matter of common knowledge, sustained by statistical record, that this level is not as high as we might like it to be. This should not be a complete surprise to us since philosophical and religious beliefs do affect conduct, ideas do have consequences. Relativism and positivism have undoubtedly affected ethics and moral conduct. When, for example, a leading scholar declares that "the seat of ethics is in the heart," and it is popular to assert that the only absolute is that there are no absolutes; when a number of religious or philosophical leaders lend their names to a declaration of their faith in man's ability "to make his way by his own means to the truth which is true to him," we should not be surprised to find some government officials making up rules which may be convenient to their own purposes and not based upon any traditional or rational standards of right and wrong, or truth and dishonesty.[3]

If we read between the lines of this quotation what we can find is a questioning attitude as to whether everything in American life is as good as it is often claimed to be, and that particularly with reference to such key sets of values as morality and religion. My own basic point, then, is that these are the very sets of values that should be examined in our schools, and not merely bypassed or ignored.[4]

At the very outset of this essay I mentioned the Notre Dame volume entitled *Values in America*. This book provides us with a further example of the sort of endeavor that should be made to bring out the good and the bad in the "American way of life." Its chapters pretty well typify the range of values in American life, as may be gathered from some of the titles as follows: "Values and Modern Education in the U.S."; "Individualism in American Industry"; "American Values in the Perspective of Faith"; "Religious Values; a Sociological Perspective." As a sample of what this particular book has to offer I quote from the last mentioned article by Joseph H. Fichter, S.J.:

The value-system of the American culture *includes* religious values in which there is a genuine "trust in God" even though the motivational attitude for this trust may often

---

[3] Eugene McCarthy, *Frontiers in American Democracy* (Cleveland: World Publ. Co., 1960), p. 75.

[4] See also my article entitled "No Wisdom Beneath the Ivy," *Catholic Mind* (March, 1963) Vol. LXI, No. 1171, pp. 47–54.

be utilitarian. . . . The point of importance here is the fact that while the American value-system is secular, it is by no means profane.[5]

As a final example of the sort of inquiry that can only lead to the more *thoughtful* development of our national life as a whole I cite the work of the *Center for the Study of Democratic Institutions* in America. This work has been carried on over a number of years under the leadership of Robert M. Hutchins, and its purpose is precisely to explore the rational foundations (where they exist) of our American society. Hutchins himself takes note of this fact as follows:

> We have engaged in our studies scientists, theologians, publishers, mathematicians, philosophers, politicians, novelists, military commentators, businessmen, doctors, lawyers, judges, teachers — men and women from every kind of background. We have secured the participation of Catholics, Protestants, Jews, secularists, men who call themselves "radicals," and others who regard themselves as "conservatives." . . . At the headquarters of the Center we meet every day to try to . . . consider possible ways of maintaining freedom and justice in a clanging, clamoring, bureaucratic, automated society.[6]

Having cited examples of the kind of self-criticism that is needed, I would submit that the continued growth of our culture in terms of an inner *meaningful* growth, a growth in depth and spiritual values, is dependent upon a continuation and more intensified pursuit of this kind of inquiry. Without the kind of intellectual leadership that concerns itself with the problem of ends or goals, our society is in danger of becoming jeopardized and controlled by the very technology

---

[5] Joseph H. Fichter, "Religious Values, A Sociological Perspective," *Values in America* (Notre Dame, Indiana: University of Notre Dame Press, 1961), p. 141. The reader may also be interested in the following quotation: "The so-called materialism of Americans is offset by their generosity, humanitarianism, sympathy for the underdog. . . . There is no need to apologize for our typical American virtues or to suppose that these virtues simply cannot be spiritually and religiously motivated." *Ibid.*, p. 144.

[6] From *The Power of Reason*, ed. by Robert Hutchins, Center for the Study of Democratic Institutions, pp. 5–6.

that we have devised as a means of alleviating the hardships of life. If the future life of Americans will be more in the tradition of leisure than of work, then it is highly important that the real meaning and value of leisure be explored by those who are best equipped to know how to handle their leisure time.

In the meantime it is the mark of a fool to imagine that the American way of life as we have known it in the past — with all of its good points and bad — should go on forever as though this way of life is an end in itself. Every man, whether he is an American or not, has a dignity and worth that make him responsible not only for his leisure time but for life as a whole. For this reason I would submit finally that the values of American life should not — all of them at least — be viewed as being man-made values and nothing more. To maintain this doctrine as Dewey seems to maintain it is to imply that *Homo Americanus* is ultimately responsible to no ends other than those which he prescribes for himself, and herein lies the essence of positivism. In contrast to such a view, I would submit that the end of the historical process lies outside of itself. Accordingly, if any particular society, such as our own, mistakes its own way of life, its own *modus operandi*, for an absolute good, it may well die on the vine. The basis of American values in the past has always been to some extent rooted in the reality of a God-centered culture. Whether such a basis is to be maintained in the future depends in large measure on the leadership of those who can show that the future of our nation lies beyond pragmatism, secularism, and positivism, in the direction of a Higher Good that no man or nation — no matter his temporal success — can prescribe for himself.

*   *   *

See also Topic Eight, No. 2;
Topic Eleven, No. 4;
Topic Eighteen, No. 5.

CHAPTER FOURTEEN

THE BEST OF FATHER VANN, O.P.

It is no small source of personal regret that one of the finest Christian philosophers of our times died before I ever had a chance to see him in the flesh. The only time I ever heard Father Vann was by tape recording one hot summer night in Texas in the studio of John Howard Griffin. Mr. Griffin had collected a number of Father Vann's tapes over the years, and it was his pleasure and mine to recapture the spirit of Father Vann in those tapes. The equipment was obsolete and the tapes were somewhat worn, but — no matter — as the basic message had gotten through as to the importance of a contemplative love of all of God's creation, of the world of things, persons, and events.

To those who knew Father Vann I can only surmise that he must have been a charming — even hilarious — individual who could extract an element of humor from the most serious situations. I forget the titles of the talks we listened to that night, but the main theme of one of them was Father Vann's insistence that "holiness means wholeness," that holiness means health and life, generosity and love. As for the books of this fine author I must confess that I have read but a few of them, though the ones that I have read are characterized by an earnestness and humor that would put most spiritual authors to shame.

In this essay I want to share with the reader a few elements of one of Father Vann's finest works, *The Divine Pity*, "a study in the social implications of the beatitudes." Take, for example, a few excerpts from his treatment of family life and the virtue of piety. Piety, as he points out, is not the sentimental thing that many persons imagine it to be, but part

of the virtue of justice, and justice in its broadest sense includes not only a desire to give others their due in a purely
legal sense but, if occasion demands, our entire selves:

> If we are Christians we dismiss once and for all the idea that
> our business in the world is to serve ourselves and nobody
> else, to become holy ourselves and pay no attention to any-
> one else. Society is for man, yes; but there is a sense in which
> man is for society too. We need society in order to grow to
> be fully men; but we need also to serve society in order to
> grow to be fully men. For without that life of service we
> doom ourselves to selfishness; and that way we shall never
> achieve wholeness.[1]

Here, then, lies one of Father Vann's main points of insistence; holiness is a kind of giving to others and it leads
to the health of the soul. The basic humanism and good
sense of the author shine forth when he applies his principles
to the concrete affairs of daily life, as when he speaks of the
need for the exercise of true piety in the home:

> We can fail in piety toward our family . . . in that sort of
> vulgarity which, because it is strident, grates upon people's
> nerves and can cause real distress, or in the type of manner-
> ism which, so far from being a charming or amusing idio-
> syncrasy, is a trial to those we live with; the priggishness
> which is a form of pride, and the snobbishness which, be-
> cause it judges people at best on unessentials, is a form of
> blindness. There is the sin of ingratitude, and taking other
> people's devotion or self-sacrifice for granted as our due.
> There is the sort of isolation which is reserve gone mad:
> you may be kindly enough disposed inside yourself, but your
> manner is such that people hesitate a long time before ap-
> pealing to you for help because you give the impression that
> you will not want to be disturbed and put out. This is akin
> to the vice of "incuriosity" of which St. Thomas treats: and
> which implies a sort of mental stagnation as far as social life
> is concerned, a lack of zest and interest which . . . denotes
> a lost childhood — the soul grown old and stale. You cannot

---

[1] Gerald Vann, O.P., *The Divine Pity* (Garden City, N. Y.: Doubleday
& Co. [Image Book], 1962), p. 61.

be living in love and piety if nothing outside yourself has interest for you.[2]

Such directness and practicality as this is found in few Christian authors who write on the spiritual life, a directness that is the product of a mind that lies in closest contact both with God and with fellowman. But there is no end to the practical wisdom of Father Vann:

> You will fail if you are glum, and never have a word of encouragement or gratitude or praise, or even a word at all, for those around you; on the other hand, you will fail if you are garrulous and boring, producing a constant stream of meaningless small talk which swirls about the heads of your relatives until they feel submerged and stifled. There is a point at which untidiness becomes a sin, because it causes real discomfort and inconvenience to others; there is, on the other hand, the finicky tidiness, the passion for quite unnecessary exactitude, which can never bear to see anything a millimetre out of its proper position, and must have every household event timed to the second, and the home itself bound tightly in domestic red tape.[3]

Alexander Pope remarks in one of his poems that "words are like leaves, and where they most abound much fruit of sense beneath is rarely found." Here I should like to cite Father Vann as an exception to Pope's rule: Father Vann is never, to say the least, at a loss for words, and his prose seems to flow on and on in a sort of endless chatter, but the kind of chatter that is fraught with the fruit of meaning every step of the way.

Having provided the reader with a sample or two of the practical wisdom of Father Vann in domestic affairs, I want now to give some insight into its yet larger perspectives, especially as they relate to the moral life of the Christian. Here let it be stated that Father Vann was an untiring advocate of an unfettered sense of morality, of a morality shot through and through with a profound sense of freedom. Al-

---

[2] *Ibid.*, pp. 63–64.
[3] *Ibid.*, pp. 64–65.

though I shall have more to say on this subject in other parts
of this work, it is worth noting, I think, that to the minds of
many persons there is a sort of incompatibility between the
practice of morality and the exercise of freedom. It is a pitiful
thing, for an example, that so many persons think that people
who are moral are "squares," with little imagination or any
real sense of understanding of people other than themselves.
To be moral is, for the most part (in this mistaken view of
what it means to be moral), to be hedged in by all sorts of
rules, laws, and regulations that restrict one's social activities
to a minimum in order to follow "the straight and narrow
path." In Father Vann's overall philosophy of life there is
no such thing as a narrow path if by "narrow" is meant an
inability to see beyond the scope of one's own nose. All true
morality is outgoing, expansive, and, like the word of God
Himself, as free as a blithesome bird. (*Verbum Dei non est
alligatum* — "The word of God is not tied down.")

What a great source of regret, therefore, that so many
young people feel compelled to reject authentic morality because they confuse it with its forbidding counterpart. Convinced in their own minds that a puritanical morality is
not for them, they go to the other extreme of leading *daring*
and *generous* but *lascivious* lives. I can't help concluding,
therefore, what a fine thing it would be if every young artist
in the world would catch something of the spirit of St.
Augustine ("Love God and do as you please"), of Thomas
Merton ("Smile, God loves you"), and of Father Vann.
Listen to what Father Vann has to say on prudence:

> Two predominant factors in contemporary Catholic thinking
> or feeling about morality are negativism and fear; and they
> are closely related. Goodness tends to be equated with (nega-
> tive) sinlessness, and therefore the main motive for doing
> this or not doing that is fear, fear of blotting this spotless
> *tabula rasa*, and the concomitant slogan is "Safety First." . . .
> And therefore prudence has come to mean quite simply,
> caution, the caution necessary to avoid all danger and ensure

complete safety. . . . Prudence, phronesis, *does not mean caution*: it means practical wisdom, the ability to make wise judgments about practical matters. And sometimes wisdom will require us to be cautious; but *sometimes it will require us to take risks.*[4]

The last words of the above quotation should be emblazoned, I think, in the heart of everyone who acknowledges himself to be a Christian. To be prudent is not to be hampered by the letter of the law, but to be ruled by its spirit, and this often involves the taking of all sorts of risks. On the other hand, to be afraid to take risks (a mentality so characteristic of "conservative" Catholics) is a habit of mind that most often serves to paralyze action when it is perfectly clear that action most needs to be taken as in defense of one's neighbor's rights. In any event it is always wrong to use prudence as an excuse for one's own lack of courage.

One other point. A mistaken notion of prudence most often leads to an unwholesome feeling of guilt when one finally *does* decide to take risks, and then the inevitable questions arise: am I *sure* that I am taking the right path, that I married the right person, that I am punishing the right child, and so on to the point of neurotic guilt. Unhappily it is not enough for such persons that sin is in some sense real, that sin exists; rather they are burdened with the subconscious conviction that sin and nothing else exists. For such persons the only sound bit of advice is this: *don't worry* about being absolutely sure. Aristotle was quite right when he said that it is unreasonable to look for absolute certainty where it cannot be had. Provided, therefore, one has acted in good conscience *at the time* he performed a given act he need have no cause for concern, and he had best relieve himself of all sense of guilt.

Having given the reader some inkling of Father Vann's notion of prudence, I want him to see now how he applies it to the realm of art. Granted that prudence and art are

---

[4] Gerald Vann, O.P., "Culture and Morality," *The Critic*, December, 1962–January, 1963, Vol. XXI, No. 3, p. 16.

different sets of virtues (the one having to do with the *doing*, and the other with the *making* of things), a close connection exists between prudence and art. A false or mistaken notion of prudence most often leads to a mistaken notion of the meaning of art:

> Prudence [that is, a *mistaken* notion of it] does not after all, have any concern with aesthetic values. . . . Again and again a great book or film or painting will be renounced as "immoral" while the mawkish, the moronic, the aesthetically meretricious will be extolled because its message is regarded as edifying or at least "safe." . . .[5]

What this quotation points up is the kind of distortion that results from a falsely construed, moralistic approach to art, leading as it does to a failure to distinguish between good and bad art. Thus:

> . . . A novel, a play or film which communicates a profound insight into the nature of the Church will be denounced because it contains a "disedifying" portrayal of a priest; another book or film on a similar theme will be praised because it makes everything in the ecclesiastical garden lovely, even though this is a falsehood and a sentimentalized picture . . . of the very stuff of religion.[6]

No doubt the real and animating source of the spiritual vitality of Father Vann was his contemplative vocation. This does not mean that Father Vann spent his days in a monastery (which indeed he did not) but that he carried his environment with him, and his environment was that of a constant living in the Presence of God. What is so remarkably attractive about Father Vann's writings is his fully integrated approach to the meaning of the contemplative life:

> A cultural renaissance must mean a contemplative renaissance, a rebirth of vision, natural and supernatural. . . . But today just as we sin against both art and prudence by being manichean negativists, so we sin against both action and contemplation by being activists. In the context of religion, contemplation primarily means prayer, and prayer is, essen-

[5] *Ibid.*, p. 17.
[6] *Ibid.*, p. 17.

tially, a loving and adoring awareness of God; and this in turn implies being *still* in order to look and listen and absorb. To the modern Catholic, on the other hand, prayer suggests activity; to "pray without ceasing" suggests saying endless prayers, engaging in countless spiritual "exercises," and the much misunderstood term "meditation" suggests a busy pursuit of some devout train of thought . . . rather in the manner of an eager terrier worrying a bone.[7]

The one line in the above quotation which enjoins one to be "still in order to look and listen and absorb" is reminiscent of the scriptural quotation etched over the famous retreat house for men at the Trappists in Gethsemani, Kentucky: "Be still and know that I am your God."

Elsewhere I shall have more to say on the meaning of contemplative knowledge, but I want to note here that contemplation to Father Vann is an activity that is open to all provided one withdraws (mentally at least) from the "rat race" of modern life. As a step toward contemplation he recommends (1) the practice of culling certain phrases that help one to think of God, and (2) the practice of handling for some few moments of the day some sensible little object, like a leaf or a cricket, even a dog perhaps, as a reminder that God is present in all things. Happily, too, Father Vann is not the sort of person who — to extol the joys of religious contemplation — feels compelled as it were to berate the value of philosophical knowledge as such. As he expresses it:

Philosophy can not only show us the ultimate *ratio*, the meaning and pattern, of created reality but also enable us to glimpse something of the divine logic from whom all meaning and pattern derive.[8]

On the other hand, Father Vann would be the first to agree that philosophy by itself *is* incomplete, and that there is a certain point at which the philosopher must acknowledge the limits of a purely rational mode of inquiry. As another fine Christian author expresses this point:

---

[7] *Ibid.*, pp. 17–18.
[8] *Ibid.*, p. 16.

There is something artificial about the distinction (between philosopher and mystic). . . . However well founded it may be, it posits the "philosopher" and the "mystic" as abstract beings. It distinguishes two functions of the mind. . . . While (these) functions are diverse, we must not forget that *the spirit is one.* No philosopher worthy of the name would be content to remain for good and all imprisoned in his specialty. . . . The philosopher is more than a philosopher, and cannot be reduced to a precise definition. His knowledge of the world is equivalently . . . the perception of his own inadequacy.[9]

In similar vein Bergson too was right in pointing to the mystics (and I consider Father Vann to be a real "flesh and blood" mystic) as the "supermen" of the race — supermen, indeed, because they rose to a level of perfection such as they could not possibly have achieved by their own purely natural resources.

There is no hope for us in knowledge if knowledge . . . becomes itself part of the rat race, the fury and folly of amassing facts and skills simply in order to "get on" in the world. Knowledge is golden only if it is primarily contemplative, if its purpose is expressed in the prayer, "Lord, that I may *see*" — that I may learn to see and love all things, and above all to see and love them as *indwelt* by you, and therefore to see you who are "all in all." Knowledge is golden when it enables a man to cry, "I know that my redeemer liveth, and that in the flesh of created reality, words, facts, truths, I can see God."[10]

*   *   *

See also Topic One, Nos. 1–13;
        Topic Twelve, Nos. 1–6;
        Topic Nine, No. 5;
        Topic Fourteen, Nos. 2, 4, 5;
        Topic Twenty-One, Nos. 1–10.

---

[9] Henri de Lubac, *The Discovery of God* (New York: P. J. Kenedy and Sons, 1960), p. 47.

[10] Gerald Vann, O.P., "Culture and Morality," *The Critic*, December, 1962–January, 1963, Vol. XXI, No. 3, p. 17.

CHAPTER FIFTEEN

VANCOUVER AND THE SPIRIT OF UNBELIEF

The wonders of air transportation have been to me, especially in recent years, a source of great fascination. Especially was this so on the occasion of a trip from my home in Kansas City to Vancouver, B. C. I had been invited by the Basilian Fathers of St. Mark's College (itself part of the campus of the University of British Columbia) to give a talk on a broad enough topic entitled "Traditions of Christianity and Modern Atheism." Leaving home after breakfast, I found myself in a few short hours traveling over the Rockies; a little later I had occasion to see from the air the splendors of Mount Hood and Mount Ranier. At four in the afternoon I had arrived in what I later came to regard from the standpoint of Canadian friends as the Pacific *Southwest.* I was greeted at the airport by one of the priests and at eight in the evening I delivered my address.

The topic of the address has given me much pause for reflection since that time, and I want to share with the reader several afterthoughts concerning this matter of belief and unbelief. Surely, a Christian philosopher is not as such an apologete, yet neither is it possible for him to bury his head as regards the unbelief that is so much a sign of our times. As I see it, unbelief is not quite the same thing as *disbelief,* insofar as the former seems to be more a *failure* to believe in the sense of a *spiritual atrophy*, a deep-down dryness of the spirit, whereas the latter is an insistent *refusal* to believe. Admittedly, a considerable number of persons refuse to accept anything on faith, on divine revelation, but they are, I think, in the minority. Doubtless the large majority of persons who have no faith are those who have more than a prurient interest in religion as they are the kind of people who would *like* to believe if in some manner someone *could show them the way*. At least they are not the kind of persons who have a closed mind. It is with respect to this type of person, I think, that the spirit of ecumenism should be extended beyond the scope of Protestants, Catholics, and Jews. It should be made to include as well all men of goodwill — whether they are believers or not. Even in the times of St. Thomas was it not customary to draw up an apologetic (a *Summa Contra Gentes*) that was meant for all outside the pale of the faith?

In his very fine book *God in Modern Philosophy*[1] Professor James Collins makes a remark to the effect that the banishment of God is the root of our cultural malaise, and I entirely agree with this statement. But I think that the problem in modern society is less one of a "banishment of God" than it is a sort of "drifting away" from God, a simple failure to see the relevance of God in one's personal life, and the reason why many persons drift from God is most often related to their personal image of God as a Great Spirit with a big stick, a tyrant God who is ready to thwart human effort, to punish, or to destroy at the slightest provocation. Be this as it may, few unbelievers are scoffers after the manner of the old-fashioned atheist who challenges God to strike him dead on the stage.

Such was not the case, at any rate, with a young lady that I met after I delivered my talk. To this young lady *it made*

---

[1] James Collins, *God in Modern Philosophy* (Chicago: H. Regnery and Co., 1959).

no great difference whether one was a believer or not, provided only that one is fair and honest with one's fellowman and subscribes to some code of ethics. Perhaps I should have remembered to say that even for William James the will to believe *does* make a difference, but as her problem went deeper than this I arranged to see her for a more extended visit on the following day.

The subject of our next day's discussion centered on the yet different topic as to whether philosophers could actually prove the existence of God. In this young lady's opinion philosophers tend only to muddy things up, and I for the most part could only agree with her except to remark that certain traditional proofs for the existence of God are pretty basically sound, once they are seen in their proper light. At this point, however, it would have been a tedious business to have gone through the five ways of Aquinas, as I have found that even a semester's work in Natural Theology has enough problems of its own. Regardless, I did try to show that the proofs for the existence of God are based, all of them, on our experience, and if anyone questioned the validity of our experience, such as the reality of the outside world, well, that would be another topic by itself. I, for one, was not disposed to overhaul the whole of epistemology within the framework of an hour's conversation.

Having left the subject of the proofs my friend and I moved into another area of discussion that centered on the subject of morality and freedom.[2] The problem of morality seemed to have had a special significance during this particular week as a locally produced movie called "The Bitter Ash" had been banned from the university campus. Briefly, the movie was banned because the citizenry felt it to be too daring an experiment in sexual morality (or the lack of it)

---

[2] I have found over a period of years that to most people's minds the existence of God and the problem of human morality are inseparably linked with one another.

for anyone, least of all the nation's youth, to see.[3] Though my friend did not bring up the subject of the movie as such, she felt that morality is, or should be, something private, a matter of one's personal judgment and experience, thinking it to be quite unnecessary and impossible for anyone or for any organization to legislate morality for the whole of mankind. As much as I could make out, she was taking a stand in favor of situation ethics. Though I agreed with part of what the young lady said, I tried to give some explanation of the basis of the natural law, showing that there is something in all men, whether they like it or not, that everyone seems to share, namely, a fundamental striving for the good — no matter in what divergent paths they seek it. Toward the end of our discussion, I could no more than hope that there was enough of a meeting of minds for something worthwhile to "stick."

Since the time of this meeting and my trip to Vancouver I have wondered more than once as to the causes of unbelief, and this is the thought that has repeatedly come to mind: Faith is a gift, it is true, but in receiving this gift one must have an open-minded outlook toward the truth wherever it lies, especially when this source lies beyond one's natural, human reach. Yet the matter is not quite as simple as all this. The great mistake of our times, it seems, is a sort of naturalism that is based on the presupposition that man is sufficient to himself, and in this presupposition he sins — consciously or unconsciously — against the light. For one thing, many persons are afraid of God, even if they suspect in their hearts that He exists, because they are afraid to give up their freedom, little realizing that it is a certain kind of surrender, a surrender of the lower self, of the ego, to another Person, to a Person infinitely higher and more perfect than themselves, that the real meaning of freedom is achieved. To borrow a

---

[3] As anyone might surmise, the censorship action became a focal point of much vehement controversy in the university newspaper.

phrase of a Jewish theologian, Martin Buber, the essence of all true religion lies in an I-Thou relationship between God and myself. Better yet, as Maritain points out, it is only in the love of God that one can find the fulfillment of his true subjectivity, because only God fully knows and loves man for everything that he truly and ineffably is as an individual person.

No doubt the real difficulty that exists in the minds of unbelievers is a *sort of mental block* that prevents them from accepting the reality of unseen things, although many other persons seem readily assured of their existence. This mental block is most often due to the supposition that believers actually go around with the vision of God in their heads, and this most obviously is *not* the case any more than Heaven (which *is* the Vision of God) is earth. I suspect, then, that a large number of unbelievers are far more envious of believers than most believers imagine them to be, envious, indeed, but for the wrong reasons. It is a miserable thing to feel that you happen to be on the outside of things (the very most important things of life) when so many persons enjoy the warmth of the fireside within. Yet the point is that believers have plenty of bad moments of their own, and even in their best moments, prayer for them is not the sheer delight that pious books often make it out to be.

I want to insist on this idea of a mental block, as the causes of unbelief have, I suspect, deep psychological roots which, once properly exposed, can be eradicated. I mentioned a moment ago the confusion in some persons' minds between faith and vision. Worth mentioning also is the distorted notion that many persons have of humility, as it is the view of many unbelievers — that they are not sufficiently good or worthy to possess the Faith, and this too is a lot of plain nonsense. The question of believing or not believing is not one of worthiness, but of openness to the light, of a certain kind of docility that is willing to accept God's Word no matter how "unworthy" one happens to be.

The importance of this point calls for further elaboration, as the problem of guilt is one that plagues the heart of contemporary man. Why do so many persons consider themselves to be unworthy? No doubt *because they have a false estimation of themselves.* True enough, a large enough category of nonbelievers are on this count as psychologically normal as anyone might be, yet there are *some* who do suffer from a sense of compunction that stifles their nature and prevents them from reaching upward toward God. The fault of these persons is their failure to know their personal worth both in their own eyes *and* in the eyes of God. By a sort of paradox they are too much attached to themselves, which is to say, their lower selves, and fearful of the idea that if at some time they do give themselves over to prayer, they will make clumsy wretches of themselves and end up in a sense of failure and embarrassment.

Of a yet different category of nonbelievers are those who suffer from a moral fault that prevents them from making any attempt at prayer due to a sort of paralysis of the will. It is easy enough, of course, to tell these people to give up their bad habits, but the fact remains that one does not give up his bad habits overnight. The eradication of bad habits, just as much as the acquisition of good habits or virtues, is a lifelong task. Even so, for a person who is deeply sincere . in wanting to believe, it is never too late to make a good start by removing (with the help of a good friend or counselor) those obstacles, *including moral ones,* that lie in one's path. The worst mistake that such a person could possibly make is the mistake of despair, and to counteract it one must be fully assured that there is *never* any reason for despair, whatever one's feelings of guilt, doubt, uncertainty, or whatever one's moral faults.

In the above paragraphs I have spoken of persons for whom a situation of unbelief is a sort of mental block that can in any case and with proper handling and good judgment be removed. What I would insist upon here, however, is that there is no single influence more detrimental to belief in one who lacks faith than to be treated by believers as though one's unbelief were of necessity a sign of moral decay. For one thing it is a mark of spiritual pride for a believer to form any judgment in his mind whereby he would place himself on the side of the "good guys," consigning all others (the world of nonbelievers) to the category of more unfortunate persons, those derelicts, for whom, alas, all hope is lost. Clearly, the effect of such an attitude on the unbeliever is to associate belief itself either with a certain type of religious pietism, or possibly to identify it with a hypocritical invention of the human mind. Though this latter misconception may be rare or almost nonexistent, it is nonetheless possible, and it is possible because believers themselves sometimes give a bad example of the practice of their belief. Further, it is simply untrue to presume that nonbelievers are immoral on account of their failure to believe. Most often nonbelievers are highly moral persons whose own personal standards of (natural) morality would put many believers to shame.

The necessity of good example brings me to the last point of this essay: although all men, believers or not, are capable of an immense amount of good that often exceeds the all-too modest estimation of their own moral selves, there is no greater stimulus to belief than what Father Teilhard refers to as the "action of the saints":

> The action of the saints, even when it is very difficult to understand, is the true "real" imposed upon us and made concrete before our eyes. It is this which must guide our every attempt to systematize, since ultimately it must strip them all. As for our speculations, they will remain sterile for ourselves as well as for others unless in our lives we conform to them, and turn them into an example for other men to follow.[4]

---

[4] Quoted by Christopher Mooney, S.J., "Blondel and Teilhard de Chardin," *Thought*, Vol. XXXVII, No. 147, Winter, 1962, p. 554.

It is not enough, therefore, for believers not to create a *scandalum* — a stumbling block that would prevent would-be believers from accepting the faith. More positively, they should provide the kind of example that would attract other men, not only to themselves, but to God. It is no mere coincidence that many men were attracted to Christianity in the first place because on the basis of what they saw for themselves they could say of the early Christians: "See how they love one another."

*   *   *

See also Topic Five, Nos. 1–9.

CHAPTER SIXTEEN

A FEW NOTES ON THE ESSENCE OF
FREE CHOICE

Presumptuous as it may seem to enter on so large a topic as freedom in an essay as brief as this, it is one — if only for reasons of its importance — that I could hardly *choose* to omit.[1] My own purpose here, however, is not in any sense comprehensive: I merely want to review some of the high-lights of a topic that is of central concern to contemporary man.

No doubt the very first question that arises concerns the meaning of freedom, and quite obviously freedom does mean different things to different people. To most persons, no doubt, freedom means almost exclusively economic, political, or social freedom — a freedom *from* one kind or another of *external* constraint. I am free, for an example, from hunger if I have enough money to buy my next meal; I am free from tyranny if I have the right to vote as I please. Further, I am free in the same sense of *external* freedom if I can choose my wife, my religion, my job, or my place of work. No need, however, to multiply instances of this kind of freedom, as none of these instances signifies the *basic* kind of freedom

---

[1] If the reader is interested in a thorough presentation of the subject, he might consult Mortimer Adler's *Idea of Freedom*, a book which, I am told, was more than five years in the making and is the result of the co-operative efforts of a large number of scholars.

that exists *within the individual person himself*. It is this latter kind of freedom I shall discuss in this essay.

Basically, then, I may be said to be free from either of two points of view: (1) from the standpoint of any outside influences that might deprive me of the use of my freedom, and (2) from the standpoint of any *internal* factors within my very person that would prevent me from making a choice. This latter kind of freedom, if it truly exists, is more fundamental, and lies at the basis of all the rest. To get a clear picture of the topic consider what it would mean to say that man is not free internally, that any "decision" he makes is *only* the result of the factors that forced him to "choose" as he did.

Unquestionably many persons hold such a view — that man is not *really* free. To defend their position they will argue that man is predetermined to do what he does either because of his heredity or his environment or both. Take a person, for an example, who is reared in the slums: what choice does he have except to follow the "patterns of behavior" that have been *forced* upon him by his environment? Except through some outside influence it becomes impossible for such a person, acting on his own initiative, to transcend the limitations of his environment. Yet even apart from the question both of heredity or environment the psychological determinists will hold that *no* man is *really* free if only for the reason that in the welter of conflicting motives that "determine our mode of response" it is the *strongest motive that always prevails*. For example, if one is hungry and food is available, one has no choice *but* to eat. The strongest motive here is one that in preference to any possible others impels one to act as he does.

Whatever may be said against the position just stated this much should be said in its favor — that it does point up the need for a *motive* in *all* of our human behavior. And this point should be duly stressed against those defenders of freedom who seem to imply that free activity — to be completely free — must be free from all motivational constraint. This last proposition, however, is ambiguous and put to the wrong use can easily lead to the denial of freedom. Clearly, if the proposition is taken to mean that free activity is, under any set of circumstances, performed without any motive at all, then the proposition is plainly false, since no man can act without some kind of motive, without some kind of attraction to the good. As the saying has it, every agent, including man, must act for an end.

Yet to stress this point — that no man can act without motives — is not to concede that *the need for motivation abolishes the very roots of freedom itself*. And this is to say equivalently that motivated activity is entirely compatible with activity that is also free. Suppose, for an example, that a man is confronted with the alternatives of working in his office or playing golf, and he decides to play golf. In *either* case he was confronted with a *motive*, but the question is whether he had any control over the motives themselves or whether the motives controlled him. If the latter supposition were true, then the person simply had to do what he did and that's an end to it. If his "decision" to play golf were not ultimately up to the man himself, he would have *deceived* himself in thinking he had a choice of alternatives — which plainly on this supposition he did not. The only remaining supposition therefore is that the man — in deciding to play golf — did so because he was free.

The case against human freedom is further weakened by our awareness of control over our motives. In other words, apart from the fact that we deliberate whenever we choose, we are also aware — however implicitly so — that we can control the very process of deliberation itself, and in so doing reflect on the very motives of our activity. Thus the man who decided to play golf as an alternative to working in his office was quite aware — and *existentially so* — of both possibilities of action. Further, in the process of deliberation he was fully aware of the advantages of either course of action, and of the impossibility of doing both. Finally, he decided for himself which of the alternatives would prevail. And how did he do this? By "playing up" the desirability of one alternative (playing golf) over the other (going to the office). Indeed, it is this very power — not only of seeing the alternative but of giving preferential treatment to one motive over another — wherein the very root of our freedom lies.[2]

Let me expand somewhat on this very last point. It is a common saying in scholastic terminology that nothing is willed unless it is known. In the context of the present discussion this would mean that there is no room for choice unless I *know* what I am choosing, which is to say unless I know the alternatives involved. In other words, the will *is* dependent on the intellect for the object or objects that it pursues. Such, however, is only one half of the picture, the other half being this: the will has a measure of control in directing the attention of the intellect to a consideration of one alternative over another, and it is in this very element of control with respect to the focusing of attention on a preferred alternative wherein the real meaning of freedom comes to the fore. A man is really free when he is free to play up one motive above another or above all the rest.

I have just focused sufficient attention on the meaning of freedom in its basic psychological sense, which is a freedom to act or not to act (freedom of exercise) or a freedom to choose within a given set of means (freedom of specification). Needless to say, all sorts of factors can prevent one from performing an action that is perfectly free, but the doctrine of free will is in no way bound up with establishing the proposition that *all* of man's actions are free. The doctrine would still hold even if many or most of them were not free. Given the fact then that some of men's actions are free — it

---

[2] In our example, the very contingency of either course of action makes it impossible for a person to see in an *absolute* sense which course of action is best. It is due to this fact — that neither course of action is a good in the absolute sense — that it becomes necessary to make some kind of choice, and the choice is preceded by a preferential treatment of the motives involved.

is quite clear that there are all sorts of factors that might tend either to modify the freedom of an act or eliminate it altogether, such as ignorance, passion, fear, or the like. Yet none of these factors may be taken as a means of abolishing man's freedom, as it is one thing to say that some of man's acts are free and others are not and quite another to say (as the determinists do) that *none* of them are ever free.

Technical as the doctrine of freedom may be, it is of central importance to the understanding of the problems of contemporary man. If man is in no sense free, then he is the victim either of his own impulses or of the external threats of his environment. The denial of freedom leads, moreover, to the denial of moral responsibility, and society itself gives strong enough testimony that in the majority of his actions at least man is morally responsible. To deny this latter proposition is to render meaningless the whole business of trying accused persons in a court of law or of sentencing criminals to prison. The conclusion of this essay then is this: with all of the emphasis on freedom, it is this most basic type of freedom — the freedom within the individual person himself — that matters above all the rest. To be free means that a man can determine for himself a given course of activity — whether any outsider attempts to restrain him or not.

*   *   *

See also Topic Nineteen, Nos. 1–6.

PART TWO · · · *REFLECTIONS*

INTRODUCTORY NOTE

Actions, it is often said, speak louder than words, and very often a few well-chosen words portray their message with a vividness and intensity that is lacking in essays or entire books. This is one reason at least for the format of the second half of this volume. Another is that the reader himself is given a greater chance to *reflect* on what he has read — especially if he suffers from a limitation of time.

In any event the following reflections are an attempt to provide further insights into some of the topics already presented in the preceding essays and several others besides. Further, the chapters that follow — where the topic is new to the reader — will help bridge the gap between a long and tedious treatment of the topic and no treatment at all. In this latter instance half a loaf is certainly better than no loaf at all. Finally, it is hoped that the reader will talk back to the author and, pencil in hand, make his own notations that may in the end turn out to be better than the original text. If such be the case, no matter; the author has borne the experience on more than one occasion of having been surpassed by his students, and if he suffers the same indignity from his reader, he will take no offense. The important thing is that there be a meeting — or even a clash — of minds between reader and author. All good reading involves some kind of encounter, of dialogue between reader and author, and it is in this spirit that I simply ask the reader: *Tolle et lege,* "Take up and read," and read in any order you please.

REDEEMING THE SENSES

1. Antiseptics and Teddy Bears

Our modern culture is altogether too antiseptic. It invites us to brush our teeth when we have hardly completed our meal and while the taste of good food is still in our mouths. What is more, it often encourages us to "bribe" our children with four-foot teddy bears when all along the child could be made much happier with a simple little toy: it is the love of the parents more than the size or the number of the toys that makes children happy.

2. Inaction

We have become a society of bench-sitters and wallflowers. The good ball players keep getting better and better, while the inexperienced become more so as the bench gets warmer and as the game draws to a close. So too at dances — the "professionals" get more exercise than they need, while those who only "stand and wait" may even forget how to walk.

3. Senseless Action

Occasionally we say of a man who pursues some insane course of action that he has "taken leave of his senses," as when a man drives down a crowded street at sixty miles per hour. Such a person acts as though he had none of his senses to guide him, as though he saw nothing and heard less, and as though both memory and imagination were blanked out. The image may be exaggerated, but what it points to is the need for the use of the senses as guideposts of oncoming danger, as practical means for determining and estimating what is good or harmful for our everyday lives. Beyond this, however, one should know that a person is capable of many senseless actions other than those that impugn his physical life, such as the failure to observe the voice of one's conscience. This is tantamount to saying that the sense life of man is, and *should* be, quite different than we find it in brutes. The sense life of brutes is related purely and simply to the conditions of their biological needs — to what is good or harmful to the organism taken as such. In man the senses — beyond their biological utility — should play a much higher role, as they should be made to "cater" to one's religious, moral, and cultural needs.

4. Crash Programs

There can be no "crash" or "speed-up" programs for restoring the senses to their proper use.

5. Good Taste

One should not try too hard to cultivate the art of "gracious living." Gracious living should be the natural outcome of good taste and good judgment in all of the affairs of life, and this is an art that cannot be taught.

6. Asceticism

True asceticism does not consist in anesthetizing one's senses and emotions, but in channeling them to the purposes of a mature human life.

7. Contemplative Knowing

Let it be said over and over again that the value of the senses should never be restricted to their pure biological utility — as though the senses were instrumental *only* to the good of the organism. The fact is that *the senses have a contemplative value of their own* — a value that is realized in the life of a child whenever it explores an object, feels it, assimilates it, gets to feel at home with it, becomes psychologically attuned to it, and so on. In this way too a person should also come to know his fellowman: he should look at him when he speaks or is spoken to, he should observe the facial gesture, be attentive to the sound of the voice, the movement of the hand, the sigh, the laugh, or what have you. Only through the use of our senses can we come to know the world of things and what for us is the yet larger world of our fellowman, his thoughts, feelings, hopes, and ambitions.

8. *Worship: Human and Divine*

Worship is divine in its object, but human in its mode, and this is to say that man is a liturgical animal. When the Church therefore enacts its sacramental rites it *invites* us to the use of our senses.

9. *The Decline of Pleasure*

The modern *misuse* of the senses has resulted in what Walter Kerr has designated the "decline of pleasure." The irony of the situation is this: contemporary man has deprived himself of the very enjoyment that he constantly seeks on a sensible plane. Lest it be thought, therefore, that a genuinely Christian ethic is opposed to the use of the senses, this point should be clearly understood: from the standpoint of Christian philosophy whatever man knows and loves must somehow come up to him through the use of his senses, and this because of the *integral* nature of man. Mark the contrast, then, between the Christian ethic and behaviorism: the Christian view is unequivocally much more of a "sense-based" approach to reality than behaviorism has ever been, for the latter view has regarded the senses as no more than instruments of biological control. In so doing behaviorism has robbed the senses both of their cognitive value and of the enjoyment that results from their proper use.

10. *Emotions and the Modern Milieu*

Although the controlled use of the emotions plays an indispensable role in the life of man, the conditions of modern society tend in a quasi-stoic fashion to repress them, and this repression leads to all sorts of problems in mental health. For an example, there is *a large difference between contemplative silence and the enforced muteness that is imposed upon man by the unhappy demands of an impersonal milieu.* Occasionally, it is good and necessary for man to display a measure of anger if the situation warrants his doing so. Further, it is important for man to know that a certain kind of fear is wholesome provided it be not compulsive or irrational. The *fear of fear*, on the contrary, has caused much fruitless anxiety and caused man to lose a grip on himself and his environment.

11. *Technology and Sense*

Contemporary man has forgotten how to make full and adequate use of his senses. Christians too often regard the senses in a somewhat puritanical frame of mind, as though the generous use of them were intrinsically linked to a life of evil. The modern pagan, too, fails to use his senses but for the reason that technology has in a manner of speaking rendered their use superfluous. *The solitary experience of eating at an automated restaurant is less than a human affair.*

12. Romance

Too many young persons today feel that romance, as involving a creative attempt to appeal to the imagination of the loved one, should be a thing of the Victorian past. Romantic love is not such an antiquarian thing as many persons think it to be, and if it were more highly regarded it could serve

as a more happy prelude to marriage than those courtships
that last but a day.

13. Temperance and the Need for Enjoyment

Temperance is rooted in the need to curb and restrict our
sensible appetites so as to place them under the effective
control of some higher power such as reason or grace. Yet
we pervert the meaning of temperance if we imagine that
its object is to rid ourselves of all natural enjoyment, such
as the enjoyment of a hearty meal or of the leisurely com-
panionship of like-minded friends. Such faulty notions as
these have led many Christians to think that Christian living
is what it was never meant to be — a joyless affair — as though
there were some contradiction between genuine sobriety and
genuine mirth.

THE CULT OF CONFORMITY

1. Christopher Dawson on Organization Men

"Our modern Western secularized culture is a kind of hothouse growth. On the one hand, man is sheltered from the direct impact of reality, while on the other he is subjected to a growing pressure which makes for social conformity. He seldom has to think for himself or make vital decisions. His whole life is spent inside a highly organized artificial unity — factory, trade union, office, civil service, and his success or failure depends on his relation with this organization." Christopher Dawson, *The Crisis of Western Education* (New York: Sheed & Ward, 1961), p. 173.

2. The "Outer-Directed" Man

The need for an interior life is most dramatically evidenced by the comparative absence of it in the lives of those persons who fail to reflect on their own experience. Carried away by an excessive activism many persons in our society pass most of their lives with very little thought about the meaning of life or of death. These persons are like a ship without a rudder which swirls with each shift of the wind. They have little built-in sense of direction as befits the nature of man, and they make very little active use of their freedom whereby it is possible for them *to direct themselves* in relation to their end. Riesman's "outer-directed" man is a creature of conformity, a cog in the technological process, a victim of the latest advertising campaign. Only to a minimum degree has such a person learned to exercise his intelligence and even when he does he restricts himself to items of comparatively minor or even trivial concern.

3. The Courage to Act

In an era of conformity very few persons try — except in some eccentric fashion — to become unique. Perhaps they are too self-conscious of the way in which other persons will interpret their motives, as when they drop a coin into the hat of a sidewalk beggar. The obvious antidote, of course, for this kind of fear is courage — of the sort by which one dares to be different. At the root of such daring is the desire to do what God wants us to do in the unique circumstances of our lives. Recall, then, this profound insight of St. Thomas: a person is the more perfect insofar as his activity springs from the innermost part of his being.

4. Originality: Inauthentic and Otherwise

The more some persons try to distinguish themselves by their gaudy mannerisms and dress, the more do they confirm the impression in other persons' minds of their being like everyone else. By contrast, a person who is genuinely unique combines his uniqueness and originality with a naturalness and ease that is difficult for any but a trained observer to detect. This is one of the reasons, incidentally, why the presence of truly great persons is often obscured in the multitude.

5. The Development of a Creative Minority

The best counterbalance for the cult of conformity in its bad sense is the development of what Arnold Toynbee has called a "creative minority." Indeed the success of every great culture, of every great civilization, has been dependent upon the dynamism and productivity of such a minority group within that culture. It is the creative minority, whether as artists, as teachers, as civic leaders, or what have you, which makes the difference between a civilization that is either decadent or mediocre and one that is alive to the challenges of its day. Such was the case in Aristotle's time and such is the case today. The problem, however, of our present-day culture is not so much how to save it, but how to provide those conditions that will guarantee the emergence of a new generation of leaders who will give it impetus and direction. The problem is to pave the way for a kind of leadership — through a creative minority — that will give our society a measure of unity that will heal the split between religious ideals (where they exist) and the world of secular endeavor.

6. Conformity Culture

A conformity culture is a good one if "conformity" here is taken to mean conformity to an objective set of standards which themselves are in conformity with the fundamental nature of man and the truth of divine revelation. Only as the result of a false sense of conformity do various disorders arise.

*   *   *

The failure to conform to objective standards that are universally true and relevant results in the construction of a set of values that is arbitrary and subjective, a set of values that represents a retreat from reality, and from the reality of the nature of man. Given such a "retreat" all sorts of complications arise, leading to one type or another of "abnormal" behavior — abnormal at least in the sense that it departs from the norm of what human behavior ought to be — as something to be kept under rational control and conformed to rational ends.

7. The Meaning of True Creativity

True creativity means being faithful to the fundamental

inspiration of our lives, and is a quality not restricted to the artist alone. However, all of us are in Marcel's view like artists insofar as "the artist does not know what he is going to do until he does it." In this sense it is important for every Christian to follow his own path, his own inspiration; it is important that he become an "inner-directed" man. What he must avoid like a plague is the *modus vivendi* of the "outer-directed" man who subordinates *himself* to the monotonous and imperious demands of a conformity culture, in the name of a false or misdirected sense of security. True and ultimate security lies in the pathway that one must choose on his own according to one's personal insights and the grace of a providential God.

8. *Philosophical Wisdom and Creativity*

Every man must be a philosopher for himself, and a person's philosophy is no better than his total vision of the truth. Admittedly, 'no man is in possession of the whole truth — only God *is* the whole truth and only God *knows* the whole truth fully and comprehensively. At best, then, every man's grasp of the truth — whether he be a farmer or philosopher — is only partial and limited, proportioned to his own capacities and the conditions of his environment.

Occasionally, however, after one has been laboring for the truth the whole of one's life, there comes a vision of truth in the sense of a unified grasp of the whole in which all the diverse elements of truth — known previously in a purely fragmentary fashion — have become dynamically and irresistibly united into a whole. Such a vision, when it comes (almost unawares) to the one who receives it, comes as a surprise . . . it carries him off his feet . . . it possesses him.

This vision is not the result of something that one plans or calculates in some cold, deliberative way. It is something that carries one off with the tide of *what is*, the real.

THE CULT OF PSYCHOLOGISM

1. *Psychologism and What It Means*

True self-knowledge, as Augustine intended it to be, is always to the good. However, there is a certain type of subjectivism — stemming from the Cartesian tradition — that involves an excessive preoccupation with the self for its own sake, a habit of mind that closes the door to the reality of *what is* outside the mind, and we may conveniently refer to this habit as the *cult of psychologism*. This habit is based on the view — anticipated by the sophists of old — that man is the center of all things — of those that *are* that they *are*, of those that are *not* that they are *not*. The cult of psychologism, focusing as it does on the ego, leads to definite types of neuroses, but it tends as well to rule God out of our thoughts and lives. (As Frank Sheed rightly contends, it is part of our mental health to become preoccupied, not with the thought of self, but of God.) In the spirit of those who are infected with this cult, God is no more than a "projection," a "father image," and in general "reality" itself is an imaginary projection of the subconscious. Accordingly, one no longer argues or discourses with a man on the basis of *what* he is saying, but only on the basis of the *psychological motivations* that prompted him to say what he did. All reality is ultimately of the nature, not of "what is," but of

128

what we make it out to be for ourselves and in accordance with our own desires. Applied to the level of religious truth, this doctrine leads to the indifferentist position that one religion is as good as any other, to an attitude of what Father John Courtney Murray has called a "bogus irenicism."

2. Psychologism and Prudence

The attempt to explain all human conduct in terms of subjective motivations alone — as though it were in no way based on the nature of man himself — has rendered farcical the traditional meaning of prudence. In its traditional sense prudence means right reason applied to the affairs of everyday life, the exercise of one's practical judgment in regard both to an objective norm and an end. In its modern setting "prudence" is no longer fettered by any "preconceived" norms or ends except those which the subject determines for himself. It is the prudence of those whose only ethics is that of a situation ethics which denies the validity of any universal norm of morality. In its most blatant form such prudence is sheer opportunism — the kind of prudence that seeks, for an example, to influence others, only for the purpose of using them as "objects," and not of respecting them as persons. Too, *prudence of this sort means a failure to disagree even when the truth of a situation demands that we speak our minds.* It is the kind of prudence that mistakingly identifies itself with caution, with the habit of playing one's cards close to the belt. Prudence of this sort is based on the view that all points of disagreement are merely technical or nominal ones: there is no dispute that cannot be "ironed out" at the conference table or over the drawing board — provided one is clever enough to devise the right name or to create the right image.

3. The Dual Cult: Psychologism and Conformity

The overweening habit of subjectivism may be partially characterized by the fact that those who are under its spell are less concerned with any wellsprings of their own personal action as "inner-directed" men than they are with the response (favorable it is hoped) that they can evoke in someone else and presumably someone who might serve their own selfish ends. *The cult of psychologism is that frivolous game of hide-and-seek in which everyone amiably agrees to disagree while in the meantime the absence of any real intellectual conflicts makes any serious disagreements impossible.*

4. Psychologism and the Method of Detachment

The cult of psychologism implies a detachment from the truth rather than commitment to it. The stance of the subjectivist is that of not becoming "emotionally" (or in any other way) involved, even if one sees a dead man in the street. It implies a deliberate attempt to refrain from making any "value judgments" except insofar as those judgments are subservient to the ends of the individual himself and in no way related to the common nature of man or of reality.

THE WILL-TO-MEANING:
THE NEED FOR A HIGHER PRINCIPLE

1. Social Solidarity

Frustration of the will-to-meaning is one of the outstanding characteristics of contemporary life. Closely connected with it, however, is the loss or deprivation of a sense of *social solidarity*. By this I mean the failure of modern society to provide the individual person with a *sense of belonging*, a *sense of participation* in the relations that he bears to the group — whether the group be as small as the circle of one's fellow employees or as large as the nation itself.[1] Everyone (whether a person admits it or not) keenly desires to feel "at home" with his fellows and to receive their stamp of approval for what he is and for what he does. If the chief or sole reward of one's contribution to society is nothing more than a weekly paycheck, then rightly may a person feel that his work has not received the measure of recognition it deserves.

2. Newman on Well-Intentioned People

"Some persons are so intemperate and intractable that

---

[1] In the Greek city-state or *polis* every citizen was expected to know his fellow citizen at sight.

there is no greater calamity for a good cause than they should get hold of it." John J. Newman, from the preface to *The Scope and Nature of University Education* (New York: E. P. Dutton Co., Inc., 1958), p. XXXV.

3. Meaning of Our Lives

A person's "life" is more than the sum total of his experiences. More accurately, a person's "life" is the sum total of all those things, persons, and events that one is interested in or excited about, in short, the sum total of *meaningful experiences.* Thus if baseball happens to be the dominating and focal point of one's interest and activities, then it is more than a figure of speech to say of such a person that baseball *is* his life. In a word, our lives are the sum total of all those things that capture our imagination, our fancy, our delight, the sum total of those things that absorb our energies, that occupy our time, that make life itself worth living for us. It is nothing more than that, and nothing less.

4. Will-to-Meaning: What It Means

Psychologists have pointed up in no uncertain terms that the most dominant craving of human nature is not pleasure, power, riches, fame, or what have you, but a motive which underlies the pursuit of all these other goods, namely the will-to-meaning. Without any attempt to define the will-to-meaning precisely I would suppose it to imply *the basic need in all of us to make our stamp on reality in terms of some good outside of and distinct from ourselves.* This means, of course, doing things that are either useful or useless, but above all committing ourselves to other persons for their own good and not for the good that we seek for ourselves. It is only thus that the individual can get outside of himself and identify himself with the interests, loves, and activities of his fellowman.

*   *   *

There is in all of us a basic yen for self-transcendence, the yen to serve some cause higher than our individual selves. The devoted actor lives for the play, the loving wife for her husband, and so on. As the saying has it, "No man is an island unto himself," and if he tries to become one he destroys himself.

5. *The Pursuit of Meaningful Ideals*

When we speak of ideals let us be careful never to conceive them in a way that is at variance with the true nature of man, since there are true and false ideals as well as those that are of questionable value or significance. What is necessary here is to get beyond the level of tabloid thinking, popular journalism, and the like to a solid understanding of the issues that underlie life's problems. Enthusiasm for the right causes, yes, but we should get an understanding of the ideas these causes represent. Social commitment, yes, but with a well-balanced sense of judgment that takes all the relevant circumstances into account. *Action without thought is meaningless, and thought without action is stagnant.*

6. *The Need for Self-Transcendence*

Just as matter itself — in spite of the dynamism of the material forms it possesses — can only *tend toward* a higher spiritual principle, so too human nature can only tend toward self-transcendence. There is here a total dependence on the part of the lower principle to become actuated from above by a higher principle distinct from itself. Thus animal nature cannot bridge the gap into the rational and the spiritual: there is the need for the infusion of a new and higher principle from above, and this implies (regarding the question of man's origin) the need for the infusion of a rational soul as a principle to inform the matter that all but reaches up to such a principle without achieving it, however, on its own.

In like manner human nature tends toward a yet Higher Principle which it cannot possibly achieve on its own — to give it a new perfection, a new orientation. In Catholic theology we recognize that this higher principle is grace, something freely given to man by God, something that elevates human nature to a point of transformation that transcends human nature, something that enables man to share in the Divine Nature.

*   *   *

The natural desire that all men have of God is a basic expression of this ontological tendency of the lower nature reaching up toward a principle beyond itself. What matters here in the practical order — i.e., in the order of what constitutes man's happiness — is the need for giving this natural tendency its "proper outlet," which is nothing less than the love of God in one's personal life.

The fundamental problem of evil — moral evil in the world — is (to speak in psychological terms) the repression of this upward tendency toward the Highest Good and the subsequent attempt to take a lower good (even if it be a rational one) as means of compensation for that which lies above it. Herein lies a source of radical disorder. To bring this truth home in very concrete terms, let us make it clear that goods of a biological order (food, sex, etc.) can never be made to substitute for those of a higher cultural plane; neither may it be supposed that philosophy (a rational good) can ever be made a substitute for religion (a supernatural good).

*   *   *

Fulfillment of the will-to-meaning (which seems to be something basic in man) is dependent on man's successful attempt to *transcend himself*, in terms of a goal that lies outside of and above himself.

*   *   *

The immanent purposefulness of the reality of being a person is something which no one can cast off no matter how hard he tries. Escape mechanisms, then, are only futile attempts to distract us from what we are and what we are for. It is impossible for us to escape from ourselves.

ATHEISM, AGNOSTICISM, AND THE SPIRIT OF UNBELIEF

1. The "Death" of God

Nietzsche proclaimed the death of God, and in a sense he was right. God is dead in society whenever those who profess belief in Him fail to exercise the intelligence and courage to make the Reality of God relevant to their personal lives and the lives of their fellowman.

* * *

Much of the unbelief of unbelievers is reenforced by various factors which accompany the belief of believers, such as their pietism, their moralism, their activism, their indifference, or even their *overbelief*. On this last point let me say this: While it is the way of modern pagans to want to see all and believe nothing, it is also the habit of many Christians, certainly Catholics among them, to want to believe all and see nothing for themselves. Needless to say, neither of these extremes is desirable.

* * *

Atheists will never be converted if Christians continue to utter pious nothings into their ears, nor will they be converted by the methods of a purely rational persuasion. What Christians must do is *to get at the subconscious motivations that underlie atheistic habits of disbelief.* Most often God is rejected, not because of disbelief in His *existence,* but because of a *scandalum* (a stumbling block) that exists in one's personal life. It is this stumbling block (most often a moral problem) that must be removed prior to a real conversion.

* * *

The frame of mind of most "practical" atheists is not one of malicious intent but of the irrelevance of religious belief — of irrelevance I might add that is partially the result of the failure of believers themselves to secure the integration between knowledge and life.

2. The Heart of Agnosticism

I have always thought that the following would be an excellent prayer for an agnostic:

> O God, if there is a God;
> Hear this prayer, if it is a prayer;
> Save my soul, if I have a soul.

An agnostic is etymologically *one who simply does not know.* It would be a mistake, however, to imagine that an agnostic is a "know-nothing." He might be a scientist of the first rank. In the technical sense of the term an agnostic is a person who disavows all knowledge of any *ultimate* truths whether of a philosophical or theological order. The reason for this sort of denial is the failure to recognize the power of human reason — with or without the aid of Revelation — to know beyond the realm of human sensible experience.

* * *

Agnosticism is an *intellectual vacuum,* and it is not for long that the intellectual and spiritual life of man can survive in such a vacuum. In the long run man must have some truths to live by, and it is a matter of transcendent importance that the truths by which he lives be other than those of his own making. There is little more, then, that we need say of the agnostic except to express the wish that he be not permanently engulfed in a world of his own where there are no ultimate truths.

3. The Rejection of the Absolute

The story of contemporary thought is the story of the denial of the Absolute of Hegel. Marx, for example, retained Hegel's historical process but made man himself — collective man — the Ultimate Goal. Nietzsche in somewhat different fashion quite prophetically, though somewhat prematurely, proclaimed the death of God — but only to erect in His place the superman who would rule the world. More recently, Jean-Paul Sartre gets rid of Zeus on the grounds that Zeus is a monstrous tyrant who deprives man of the one thing precious to him — his freedom. The story, then, of modern atheism is the story of the rejection of Hegel's Absolute God.

4. The Undermining of Christian Culture

To understand the full impact of the contemporary history of Christianity we do so against the background of the sustained attacks that have been waged against it since the days of Nietzsche and Marx. Together with the proclamation of the death of God both of these men were intent on destroying Christian culture together with the "slave morality" that it represented to their minds.

But it is not enough merely to view Christianity from the standpoint of the attacks waged against it by atheists. We must view it also from the standpoint of its own weaknesses and failures to measure up to the challenges of the new era — Christianity's failure to appreciate the rise of science, the arts, in short, all the new forces that have shaped modern society as we know it today. The problem, then, of trying to show the relevance of Christianity today is in part the problem of making a unified attempt to adapt to all the best elements of modern culture together with the effort of purging modern culture itself of what is alien to the best interests of man. It is the problem of making up for lost time.

5. Sources of Unbelief: Historical Background

The middle ages was an era of rogues as well as of saints, and the "common man" knew quite little about his religion in the thirteenth century. Even so, what he did know was an integral part of his life, and at any rate the air that he breathed (unlike that of the present era) was not one of agnosticism, or worse, of sustained attacks against his belief in God.

In more recent times, if by "recent" we mean the period since Descartes and the advent of modern science, the influence of religion as a dynamic factor in society has begun to decline. This period of decline came to a head especially in the nineteenth century both in Europe and in America. Not that the nineteenth century was one of a complete eclipse of the Christian spirit, but rather that during this period Christianity was under open attack. This was the era in which the atheist gained a respectability he seldom if ever previously enjoyed, in which atheism itself, like that of Nietzsche, became a sort of religion of its own to compete on open grounds with Judaism and Christianity.

6. Militant Atheism

The position of the atheist is that of a commitment to unbelief. An atheist, unlike a simple agnostic, is not one who to his own mind does not know. Rather he is one who knows that he is right and that others, namely, the world of believers, are wrong. An atheist, if he is sufficiently strong in his disbelief, is committed to *the belief in the ability of man to choose his own way without God*. Naturally enough, some atheists would rather play badminton than pray, and suffer no pangs of conscience as a result. They are the kind who simply don't believe in God and that's an end to it. Others, however, are far less content to leave God alone. God doesn't exist for them, to be sure, but all the while they feel constrained to fight God and possibly also those who believe in

God. It is this latter type which stands a far better chance in the long run of becoming a theist if only for the reason that in his very profession of denial he can't seem to leave God alone. Here, as in human affairs, *it is easier to love him whom you hate rather than the one you choose to ignore.*

7. Reflections on Sartre

Sartrean man is a committed individual, it is true, but he is as much committed to his pride as he is to his freedom. He is the sort of person who looks with contempt on an attitude of humility before being, who refuses to accept *that* salvation which Christ offered to all *because* it is offered to all. He is a do-it-yourselfer all the way.

*   *   *

The atheism of Sartre represents itself as a form of humanism. For very passionate reasons God can't exist for Sartre because the Absolute, like an invader or an intruder, would destroy the realm of true subjectivity for man. Unhappily, there exists in Sartre's mind the *false dichotomy between God and human freedom.* This dichotomy rests on the faulty assumption that God, if He were to exist, would allow man no room for any thought or action of his own. On this point Maritain better than anyone else perhaps has shown the absurdity of Sartre's fundamental assumption. The assumption is absurd because of Sartre's failure to know that the real, existential God of the Jewish and Christian tradition is a God who more than anything else knows and loves man *as a subject*, which is to say, in his true subjectivity. If, therefore, one speaks of such a God as "dominating" man, this must be understood in the higher sense of *the surrender of Christian love.* If God dominates man, He does so by the exigencies of an inner inspiration that impels and motivates man to put his freedom to its highest possible use.

8. Rejection of God

From the standpoint of ontology, the great source of human unhappiness in the world of today is the contemporary rejection of God — either in theory, in practice, or in both. The remedy lies in a return to the Living God.

9. Practical Atheism and Its Cure

Practical atheism is less a positive and dogmatic denial of God than it is a forgetfulness of God characterized by a cloud of nonmystical unknowing. It is not a logical proposition, but a state of mind — a sort of spiritual torpor — engendered by a false sense of autonomy and an inadequate understanding of the ultimate meaning and purpose of human life.

*   *   *

What modern atheists need is a spirit of openness to the light. This spirit of openness, however, is hardly generated in an atmosphere in which the world of believers habitually give the lie in their lives to what they profess in their belief.

THE CULT OF FALSE MYTHS

1. The Esoteric and the Exoteric

Some persons like to indulge their whims in one form or another of theosophy or natural mysticism. These persons mistakingly imagine that they can, as it were, save themselves by a sort of natural technique, as though they were able to lift themselves up by their own bootstraps — without the aid of divine revelation or divine grace. Then there are others who, like the ancient Pythagoreans, think that salvation lies in philosophy. Persons of this sort might well take to heart the experience of one of the great early Christians, Justin Martyr: having sought in vain for a philosophy that would provide him with a way of life, he finally embraced Christianity. Having embraced Christianity, he found that the *Christian Faith had answered his problems better than any philosophy did or could have done.* Nor did he suppose that the way of salvation was not open to all. As a true Christian, Justin Martyr knew that it was, and it was a credit to his own humility not to reject Christianity *because* it was open to all.

2. Contemporary Life: False Myths

"The exclusion of the religious element from cultural life must of necessity leave a void; for *religion just as much as*

141

speech or culture belongs to the totality of human nature.
This void is genuinely felt and so the soul seeks more or less
consciously for some values to fill it. . . . When Science and
all other means fail to fill this void, then the religious factor
is preserved but generally applied to some false object. In
the place of religion one has an unsound mysticism, in the
place of God, an idol. Where there is no faith, there must
be superstition, and where God is not, then spirits rule.
*Such things as theosophy . . . occultism, and spiritism rise
up out of the ruins of religion."* Arnold Rademacher, *Religion
and Life* (Westminster: Newman Press, 1962), p. 62.

*   *   *

"The incapacity for straight thinking on moral and religious
ideas, found today even in the most cultivated circles, is only
an external symptom of the spiritual degeneracy of those who
have lost sight of the intimate bond between religion and
life." *Ibid.*, p. 59.

*   *   *

"Religion is the right relation of man to God, and so it
addresses itself to the whole man, just as life also claims the
whole man. Religion seeks to rule man in all his energies
and purposes, as well as in all his human relationships. It is
not just one aspect of the life of the spirit, nor is it confined
to one faculty of the soul. . . . Religion is incomplete without
culture. It seeks to pervade all relationships; it does not build
on nature as on a foundation, but raises it up and realizes its
true being." *Ibid.*, p. 63.

*   *   *

"Culture alone cannot fulfill man's needs and so cannot
make him happy, and it is a remarkable fact that after a
period of climax in purely human culture there is always a
period of cultural pessimism: that this should be so is no
accident but a consequence of the intrinsic nature of the
human soul." *Ibid.*, p. 63.

3. God and Human Myths

Nature abhors a vacuum and this holds true for human nature as well. If men, therefore, for one reason or another deny the existence of God, they do so to exalt some other type of good that is not God. The problem here is that of *the substitution of the so-called "myth" of God with the real myth that something other than God can bring genuine happiness to man.* Needless to say, there is no greater lie that man can tell himself than to say (in whatever fashion he says it or for whatever reason) that there is no God. It is this denial, however, even though it be made on no more than a practical level through a forgetfulness of God, that is the ultimate source and root of all the unhappiness that tugs at the heart of contemporary man. Given this fundamental denial it becomes impossible (metaphysically and psychologically so) for man by whatever techniques, distractions, escape mechanisms, and the like to find any lasting satisfaction or peace. As Francis Thompson expresses it: "*All things betray thee who betrayest me.*" Let it be said, then, that every escape from reality, especially from the reality of God, involves the making of all sorts of myths, but *the worst myth of all is that of the complete autonomy of the human self.*

4. False Magnanimity

Failure to reach the true goals of life takes many forms and often leads to bizarre extremes. Witness, for an example, the perverted attempts at magnanimity displayed by those persons who erect fantastic buildings which in the end are no more than dead, hollow monuments to their own egotism. Frequently too, this sort of "magnanimity" is accomplished by means that were used to cheat the poor of their meager inheritance in life, the reward of their daily labor.

GOD AND THE UNCONSCIOUS

1. The Natural Desire for God

The desire to see God — to become united with Him, the magnetic attraction of the Divine Goodness — this is a natural desire that is rooted in the very subconscious depths of the human spirit. It is the repression of this ontological longing for the Infinite that has induced a spirit of unhappiness in modern culture and modern life.

*   *   *

The problem today as in Tertullian's time is to locate a common ground within our very humanity between the believer and unbeliever with respect to the presence of God in the soul. The appeal here is less to the conscious level of reason than it is to the deep-rooted craving of the human soul itself for God and the things of God as a means of resolving inner conflicts that cannot be satisfied by finite goods. God alone can satisfy the cravings of the human heart for happiness — and these cravings are as deep-rooted as God Himself is in the inner depths of our own unconscious.

2. The Presence of God and the Unconscious

The mistake of Freudian naturalism has been the reductionist mistake of reducing the Higher Principle to the lower, of consigning the Reality of God to the level of a subconscious myth, of a mere psychological phenomenon. The mistake, on the other hand, of many believers has been the failure to see the reality of the Divine Immanence, the Presence of God within us, especially within the very depths of the Ego.

On this point every Christian should take a lesson from the great mystics who were aware at each moment of the Presence of God in the depths of the human soul. Did not St. Augustine discover God in the depths of the unconscious when he exclaimed: "You were there (within me) all along, and I knew you not"?

3. God and the Human Psyche

Catholic philosophers and theologians have tended in the past to ignore the unconscious and the irrational as a real source of motivation in human behavior and to this extent committed themselves to a type of pure metaphysical rationalism. Thinkers like Freud, Schopenhauer, and Nietzsche, on the other hand, tend to stress what they regard as the primacy of the irrational in all human thought and behavior. Even God Himself in Freud's view is a psychological projection of the father image, a myth that springs forth from the unconscious. Such thinkers as Freud have prepared the way for what in modern times is the cult of psychologism. What is needed, therefore, in the realm of Christian thought is a type of intellectualism that balances off the rational and the irrational in human behavior, a kind of intellectualism that takes into account both the conscious and the subconscious element in human behavior. Thus, for an example, it is fully true that God is *He Who is* but it is also true on a psychological plane that *God is present to me even in the sub-soil, in the depths of my subconscious.* He is not or should not be a surface "thought" on the abstract level of consciousness alone.

4. Man and His Need for God

Whether man experiences it or not his greatest need in this life is the need for God. Few people, of course, are absolutely convinced of this truth and even those among them who are must continually remind themselves of the Presence of God in their souls. Man is by and large an earthbound creature, and it is the rare type of individual who conforms to Bergson's magnificent ideal of the mystic and the saint. Unfortunately, the religious ideal of total dedication and service to God is for most persons an ideal that is seemingly too remote to be capable of achievement.

Yet, despite all this, the fundamental truth of man's need for God remains unaltered, and the sooner any individual comes to grips with this need, the better it will go for him and his neighbors. The knowledge of one's need for God is the first step toward a radical conversion. Unfortunately, however, contemporary life is plagued with all sorts of distractions and escapes, and *it is quite easy to become so fascinated by artificial values of a questionable nature that one loses sight of the most basic natural ones*, and herein lies the problem of contemporary man.

*   *   *

Contemporary man, by and large, has lost sight of his most basic natural needs but especially of his need for God. The great problem, then, of contemporary life is not the so-called "problem of God." God is not a problem, least of all to Himself, but man is. Man is a problem because having lost sight of God he has also lost the sight of his most basic Need — the nonfulfillment of which can and does lead to every possible kind of frustration, unhappiness, guilt, and anxiety.

*   *   *

It was to the credit of Freud that he understood something of the subconscious basis of all human activity, including religious worship itself. His great fault was his failure to know the ontological content of religious belief. Many Christians, therefore, could stand Freud on his head if they were to know that the roots of religion should be found in the very subconscious depths of their being. Their fault is to confine religion to pure rational consciousness alone — a consciousness that has no profound effect on their personal lives.

THE SPIRIT OF PRACTICAL NATURALISM

1. *Weigel: On Naturalism, Asceticism, and Faith*

"Naturalistic secularism . . . is the privileged theology of our land. . . . No one has given us a systematic expression of this theory but elements of it are clear enough. It is an amalgam of scepticism, empiricism, and pragmatism. It despairs of knowing reality in itself and restricts its knowledge to what is experienced. . . . There is here no room for God as the holy. . . . But unlike other naturalisms of the past, our naturalism has no quarrel with religion. With condescension it treats it as a sociological psychological phenomenon. For naturalism there is no less truth in Hottentot worship than in Christian cult." Gustave Weigel, S.J., *The Modern God* (New York: The Macmillan Co., 1963), p. 32.

*　　*　　*

"At times one wonders if the intellectuals of our moment do not simply take the philosopher's absolute and cover it with the robes of God. It is hard to see that the God so many of our modern prophets proclaim loves us or cares about us. For many he seems to be something away off in outer space so that we cannot see him at all and we must content ourselves in knowing that he is there, although we can never really know him as he is." *Ibid.*, p. 93.

147

*   *   *

"The girding of lean loins for battle is put off until war is already declared. . . . But training is hard and only some kind of Puritanism, stoic or Christian, can make it palatable. Our flight from Puritanism renders us collectively incapable of the rigors of training. The modern concern for dieting is a strange phenomenon in a world where almost two-thirds of mankind are underfed. *And in our dieting we all look for a regime which will work without willpower and we want to become slim not because it will make us stronger for work and endurance but for esthetic reasons. We diet, but we do not fast.*" *Ibid.*, p. 141.

*   *   *

"If cultures are in conflict, the radical conflict is in faith. Every culture rests ultimately on its faith. . . . Such faith is undoubtedly an intellectual achievement but there is a strong element of will behind the intellectual assent. There is no faith where there is no will to believe. . . . When times are good and life is easy, faith is not tested. It is in crisis and hardship that the caliber of faith is evident. It is faith that moves mountains, a feat today less impressive than the endurance of stretched-out suffering. Faith has as one of its meanings, steadfastness. *To be steadfast to vision is the mark of strong faith.*" *Ibid.*, p. 14.

2. The Naturalistic Drive

The spirit of practical naturalism may be summarized in not too many words. In many persons this spirit is characterized by the unmitigated pursuit of sensible goods, not for their own sake, or even for the sake of the pleasure they bring, but for the sake of impressing one's neighbors with one's own superiority of economic status, taste in dress, cultural values, and the like. The spirit of naturalism, especially in America, is characterized by a theoretical assent to the maxim "In God we trust" and by a practice that gives lie to the theory. In more recent times it is symptomized by a crash-program mentality. Many persons fail to recognize that *one of the most basic needs is the need for taking one's time.* For them human life itself becomes a crash program that is most often geared to a premature death. The energies for external works are boundless, but the realm of contemplation, of an intense interior life, evokes little or no response. As the expression goes, it "leaves them cold."

* * *

"Modern man *lives* according to the principles of self-denial and *thinks* in terms of self-interest." Erich Fromm, "Selfishness, Self-Love, and Self-Interest," *An Outline of Psychoanalysis,* ed. by Clare Thompson (New York: Modern Library, 1955), Ch. 20, p. 333.

* * *

The spirit of naturalism in modern life has identified itself less with a spirit of responsibility than with a spirit of intense and even, at times, ruthless competition.

There is no question here of the legitimate and reasonable desire to maintain one's self-respect, habit of neatness, and the like. Industry and self-reliance are virtues. What is reprehensible, however, is the desire to prove one's superiority over one's fellowman at whatever cost. Thus there are countless persons in our society who feel, as it were, an inner compulsion to improve, not themselves, but their *status* to the point where their superiority in all things will remain unchallenged. This spirit of competition — which is rooted in human pride — is not confined to the business world alone, for it is prevalent as well in social and cultural affairs. Thus it often becomes a matter of supreme "cultural" importance to have the "right" book, or to have seen the "right" play or musical; it is important if one wishes to make the "right" contacts to know the "right" people who belong to the "right" club, who live in the "right" neighborhood, who go to the "right" school, or even to the "right" church. The *obvious meaning of the term "right" in all of these uses is taken with reference* not to one's own personal judgment as to what is best in itself and in terms of its own merits, but of what is socially approved by the "right" people — who belong to a privileged caste.

GOD AND THE HUMAN ENCOUNTER

1. Mental Health and the Presence of God

"To know that God is and that He is everywhere is part of mental health." This saying of Frank Sheed's may not be obvious on the surface. Some people, after all, seem to get along quite gloriously without God and suffer very little mental strain as a result. Yet the truth of the matter is that mental health is seldom so obvious as it is in the lives of the saints. The reason? Simply that nothing gives greater *unity* and *purpose* to our lives than does the knowledge and love of God. To the extent that anyone lacks this unity and purpose his mental health is in danger. It is for this reason that the knowledge and love of God is the most absolute guarantee of our mental health.

2. God: The Inescapable One

To say that God is He Who Is implies an "encounter" with God on the part of everything that exists. Not that anything can, as it were, "stand up" to God as though to challenge the supremacy of His rule. The encounter rather is an ontological one of complete and utter dependence. God is in such a way that He is *The Inescapable One*. Though in no sense identified with any of the things He makes, He is yet everywhere present to them, especially to man. True enough, some men — perhaps the majority — try to run away from God on a *psychological* plane, but they can never do so on the level of their *ontological* dependence. They depend upon God whether they choose to think about Him or not, and the servitude of their being implicitly forces them to gravitate toward Him as the Source of their happiness and life.

*   *   *

Man is faced with God in the very act in which he denies or tries to ignore Him, which is to say that there is in the heart of man an unrest, a metaphysical unrest and anxiety, that gives one the feeling of futility in any attempt to escape from the Absolute. Here be it stated, however, that the Absolute is never what so many persons fear — an impossible tyrant that makes impossible demands. The only demand that He makes is that of a complete surrender of self. Rightly, then, may God, even as we discover Him in philosophy, be compared to Francis Thompson's "Hound of Heaven."

3. Human Restlessness and the Divine Immutability

Man is not only a biological animal whose sole or chief orientation is toward sensible good — He is a happiness-seeking, *God-seeking animal* who finds no rest until his appetite for the good is satiated with nothing less than the Infinite Good Itself.

*   *   *

The immutability of God means not only that God does not change but also that He is the only ultimate Term of all movement and rest. This truth was dramatically expressed by St. Augustine when he acknowledged that *the human heart is incurably restless until it finds its rest in God.* If we wish, therefore, to get a profound understanding of human restlessness, we should interpret it as a sign of man's onto-logical exigency for the One Immutable God. In proportion as man removes himself from God as his End he experi-ences within himself a gnawing sense of restlessness which (far from becoming satiated by temporal good) becomes all the more intolerable and intense with their abuse. In the measure, however, in which man comes closer to God he experiences a sense of peace and contentment that participates somewhat in the Immutability of God Himself.

4. God and His Universal Presence

To say that God is everywhere and is in all things is not to utter a pious platitude but a metaphysical truth. To know this truth is to know also that God is not, as it were, a far-flung chimera, a myth, or a symbol, but a Reality and a Presence who consistently re-creates and conserves my being.

*   *   *

Herein lies a great truth: God is intimately present to a man whenever that person makes an honest effort to be present to God — both through knowledge and love. It is in the upward ascent of the mind to God in prayer — in silent prayer whether thoughtful or thoughtless — that man secures union with God.

5. Gerald Vann on Total Involvement

"As birds in the air, as fishes in the sea, so is the spirit of man in the infinity of God. We must not think of God as though he were wholly remote from us, we here, he there, as two objects face one another in their separateness. In the infinity of God we live and move and have our being. But we can forget all this, and then it ceases to be a reality for us; and we live, not the fullness of life, but only a sad sort of half-life, active on the surface, but underneath lost and silent and dead. Yet it is not easy to know the God who is in us and about us. What must we do? First, we must try to find God in the depths of our own souls. It means that every day we have to set aside for a short period the ordinary superficial things that keep us busy; we have to learn to be humble and still and adoring. . . . But there is also the second way. . . . All the things we see and love in our daily lives, the grass and the trees and the animals, these too are made by God and loved by him and are redolent of his presence. And so we have to train ourselves to realize that too. . . . Till you can sing and delight in God you can never enjoy the world. . . . If you learn to associate things with the infinite Love that made them, they will speak to you of it." Gerald Vann, O.P., *Awake in Heaven* (New York: Longmans, Green and Co., 1948), pp. 28–29.

*   *   *

"The philosophical search for God is not complete without — and indeed is meant to lead up to — the search that has to go on in the heart. *Rational knowledge is perfected when it becomes also love-knowledge;* and that implies a personal relationship, and personal relationships are made and not born. . . . So . . . with God; you have to get to know him, to realize gradually his presence in you and in the world; follow, at however respectful a distance, the mystics in their life of prayer, even if at the beginning you are more or less praying to an unknown God. . . . Train your sense to love the beauty of truth and goodness, not the shoddy and sham; *try to make your emotional life the partner and not the rival of the life of the spirit;* then you will acquire a greater directness and sureness of intellectual vision, and you will advance in wholeness . . . because then you will know in your bones that God is not a remote abstraction . . . but an immediate and compelling presence, pressing in upon you on every side like the air you breathe. . . ." *Ibid.*, pp. 40–41.

SECULARISM AND THE CHRISTIAN INTELLECTUAL

1. The "Triumph" of Secularism

Due often to the failure of Christians, the responsibility of molding contemporary life, thought, and culture has been preempted by secularistic naturalists who have convinced themselves and many others that traditional wisdom has been outmoded by the new era of science and technology. In such a view, traditional philosophy, religion, and culture are to be relegated to the purely subjective level of "value-traditions" whose sole foundation in reality is the psychological tendency to objectify one's personal ideals. To counteract such a doctrine as this it is incumbent on the Christian intellectual to show *the relevance of metaphysical wisdom to the issues of contemporary life.*

*   *   *

It is not by any superior merits of its own that the secularistic view of the world has prevailed in our times. Secularism rather has triumphed by default. It has triumphed because of the divisiveness of God-fearing people. It has triumphed too because Christians of various denominations have failed in the past to show the relevancy of their traditions to the problems of contemporary life, to the problems of art, culture, the things of the intellect, and deeper aspirations of the human soul.

2. On Being a Christian Intellectual

It is high time for Christians to foresee the ideas of their times rather than embrace them after everyone else has discovered the element of truth they contain. Why does it so often happen that Christians, who should be the true revolutionaries, are the worst reactionaries of all? By what sort of compulsion-neurosis are so many Christian intellectuals impelled to be the last soldiers to die in battlefields that are foreign to their own tradition, while they are antagonistic to causes that are spiritually allied to their own?

3. Religion and Intellectuals: Herberg

"It is no longer self-evident, especially among the younger generation and more sensitive people, that religion is simply emotion without intellectual content. On the contrary, the religious thinkers of today . . . as Maritain, Berdyaev, Buber, Tillich, Niebuhr . . . enjoy a remarkable prestige as vanguard thinkers, not only among 'religionists,' but particularly among those concerned with 'secular' interest. . . . Religion, yes, theology, is recognized as having its intellectual relevance and no institution of higher learning can be said to live up to its responsibility if it does not take this fact into account." Will Herberg, "The Making of a Pluralistic Society — A Jewish View," *Religion and the State University* (Ann Arbor: University of Michigan Press, 1957), p. 39.

GOD AND PHILOSOPHY

1. Who Is God?

When we talk about God we must be sure to whom we refer when we pronounce that sacred word. Thus the God of the eighteenth-century deists is quite different from the God of the devout humanists of a yet earlier period. The God of Søren Kierkegaard is in its turn different from the God of Hegel against whom Kierkegaard so violently reacted. The finite God of William James is different too either from the God of Hegel or of Kierkegaard or the father image of Sigmund Freud. In every instance, therefore, we must be clear on what we are talking about when we talk about God.

2. Collins and the Absolute of Hegel

"From the time of Feuerbach onwards, it has been fashionable for naturalistic humanism to protest against 'the tyranny of the Absolute.' . . . But this protest is often expanded to include a rejection of God and theistic religion. . . . Here naturalistic humanism forgets that the Hegelian absolute is at odds with the religious view of God as the supremely personal Being . . . *the tyranny of the Hegelian absolute is even more intolerable to the theist than to the naturalistic humanist.*" James Collins, "God as a Function in Modern Systems of Philosophy," *American Philosophers at Work,* Sidney Hook, ed. (New York: Criterion Books, 1956), p. 205.

3. *Jolivet and "The Crisis of God"*

"Pascal says of the God of Abraham, Isaac, and Jacob, we can only seek him with groans, that is, by a complete and painful opening of the soul and a profound humility, and this already applies to the discovery of the God 'of philosophers and scholars.' He only reveals himself to the poor in spirit, he is a presence more than a reason, and a gift more than a conquest." Regis Jolivet, *The God of Reason*, trans. by Dom Mark Pontifex (New York: Hawthorn Book Publ., 1958), p. 120.

*   *   *

"In the words of Le Senne, we find that 'God is at a crisis.' He is so in many ways. *In our thought* which is false to him through its inability to conceive him in his infinity. *In evil and in pain*, which raise problems in our hearts. *In history*, which denies him by injustice and wickedness. *In our lives*, which witness against him by our sins. But this 'crisis' of God cannot serve as an alibi for us. For God does not go bail for our idleness and hypocrisy. It is not his business to reassure us; he is our consolation, but also our goad. He is for us both peace and war, light and darkness, tranquility and anxiety, life and death, present and absent, close at hand and far away. He includes all contradictions, since he resolves them all. The apparent strength of atheism is that it grasps the negative; its obvious weakness is that it grasps nothing else. But our unhappiness . . . lies in surrendering to the negative and helping atheism to establish itself there. Our unhappiness lies too, in failing to understand that, as Christ . . . is in agony until the end of time, so too, on the plane of natural reason, *God is always 'at a crisis,' in the sense that belief in God must always be won again* . . . in spite of the obstacles which it encounters, of the scandals which it raises, and in general, in spite of all the negation which accompanies it in our finite state." *Ibid.*, p. 124.

4. Dependence on God

The starting point of all human peace, the only condition that makes it possible for man to live with himself, is for him to acknowledge the source of his radical contingence and his total dependence on God. It is this fundamental posture of "humility before being" which is a *sine qua non* for making any progress in finding one's happiness in life.

5. Thoughts from Jean Danielou

"The error of all rationalism is that of putting God on the the same basis as other objects of reason, higher, no doubt, but not really other. To paraphrase Gabriel Marcel, God cannot be treated as a problem. He represents the boundary of reason. His dazzling light prevents the eye from seeing Him. Consequently, all that we say of Him is inadequate. He cannot be contained by any concept. But at the same time all that we say of Him is true." Jean Danielou, S.J., *God and the Ways of Knowing*, trans. by W. Roberts (New York: Meridian Books, Inc., 1957), p. 62.

* * *

"[God] is, above all, the one whom I cannot make use of. The error of false philosophies is precisely that of making God an object, of claiming to possess Him through the intellect. But that which the intellect possesses could not be God. On the contrary, it must be said that the encounter with God drives the intellect to a fundamental conversion, to a decentralization from the self; and this conversion is the knowledge of God Himself. For God can only be broached as an existent and as a personal existent. . . . *To know God is not, then, to hold Him in my intellect, but on the contrary to rediscover myself as measured by Him.* . . . (Thus) the knowledge of God is a work of reason and a challenge to reason." *Ibid.*, pp. 64–65.

* * *

"When it is said that God is personal, it seems that with His transcendence what is meant above all is that it is possible to enter into communication, into communion with Him. It is just in this that the God of true philosophy is to be contrasted with the impersonal God of idealism, and even with the God of Aristotle and Plotinus who is indifferent to the world. This prepares the way for the revelation of the God of Abraham who 'speaks' to His people, who governs them, who *enfolds them in His Love*." Ibid., pp. 78–79.

THE DIMENSIONS OF CHRISTIAN MORALITY

1. Morality: True and False

A Christian approach to morality should never be a scolding, voluntaristic approach which only blames us for the wrong that we do, which points out the mistakes we have made. This we know all too well and for anyone to remind us of our mistakes is to pour salt into the wound. What is needed, then, is to help others and ourselves to see the positive in things, to become convinced of our inherent worth, of our ability to transcend ourselves.

*   *   *

Against the repressions of many false systems of morality such as we have known them in the past it is of great practical importance to the modern Christian to know: (1) that he can be moral without being dull; (2) that he can be artistic without having to preach; and (3) that he can make a bold and generous use of his senses without putting them to the service of sin.

2. Morality and Good Company

The mere fact that a person is committed to a good cause is no guarantee of the morality of the person who associates himself with that cause. Good men keep good company, it is true, but this does not imply that they are good because of the company they keep nor does it imply that the bad are never to be found with the good. Indeed, only in such exceptional societies as in a community of monks is it fairly safe to assume that only the good are present, even if not all of the good are the best. Most societies are an admixture both of the good and the bad, and a democratic society is no exception. What this amounts to in practice, then, is that identification with a good cause does not *eo ipso* make a person to be good. To be good a person must commit himself as an individual to the responsible use of his freedom for a good end.

3. Morality as National Defense

Perhaps we have reached a point in our national life of realizing (if only to a minimal degree) that a return to morality is a necessary factor for survival — as necessary as it is to arm ourselves against any external threat. Morality is the one great defense of the nation against its possible future collapse, it is a hidden reserve that guarantees a people's survival.

4. Breakdown of the Older Morality

As we witness the breakdown of the older morality — puritanical in spirit — voluntaristic in tone — dualistic in its view of man — we should not suppose that the only alternative to this older morality is no morality at all. A presupposition as faulty as this can only open the door to a society without order, to a society in which the use of human freedom becomes identified with its capricious misuse.

5. Duty for Duty's Sake

The influence of Kant's categorical imperative — duty for duty's sake — has inflicted great psychological harm on the lives of many individual Christians. What Kant should have stressed, as did both the Orientals and the Greeks, is the need to secure within ourselves an inner harmony — of the soul and with its powers, of ourselves with nature, and of each person with his fellowman. To achieve this harmony is to be moral, not only with our will, but with our whole being. Further, man must purge himself of the monstrous idea that the pathway to holiness is misery. God does not want man to be miserable, either in this life or in the next. True enough, the performance of a difficult task may not always be pleasant, may even cause a great deal of pain. Yet, if a difficult task is performed from a *motive of love* — and not merely out of a *sense of duty* to the law — it can provide a deep sense of happiness within. Deep down a person should be happy to be performing a good work because he does it, not from a sense of compulsion, but *freely* from a motive of love.

6. Art and Morality

Too many Christians in this country have failed to appreciate the aesthetic dimension of human existence. Through an overriding ethical concern, they have failed to appreciate art, the theater, good literature, and music. They have failed to realize that true morality is based on a realistic assessment of the total nature of man considered from every legitimate point of view. They have failed to realize too that nothing can so dehumanize and demoralize the creative efforts of man the artist as an overriding concern with morality in its narrower sense as though there were nothing else in the world that really mattered at all.

*   *   *

When movies and plays are poor it is not generally because of poor technology, but because of a radical ignorance on the part of writers and producers themselves of the deeper aspirations of man. This is not to say that it is the duty of the artist or writer to preach human nature. No artist as such is commissioned to preach. Yet the canons of good art require the artist to show *by means of his art* that he knows something about man as he *is*, and not as he is often imagined to be as a high level animal or brute.

There is, then, a false optimism (as in Rousseau) and a false pessimism (as in Hobbes) about the nature of man.

Yet the more common error of our day, especially in the field of drama, is to imagine that a "realistic" approach is equivalent to the assumption that man cannot rise above "himself," meaning by this, his lower inclinations or tendencies. Witness here the preoccupation of so many writers with the tawdry and sordid for its own sake. True enough, "realism" of this sort coupled with heavy-handed salesmanship and publicity often insures a good popular market. Yet the economic rewards of this kind of "literature" and drama are hardly an excuse for its flagrant violations of the canons, not only of sound morality, but of sound art. Indeed, novelists and dramatists have a particular obligation and responsibility within their profession to uplift the level of culture by good entertainment that refreshes, purifies, and restores the energies of the soul.

FAITH, REASON, AND CULTURE

1. Rationalism and Fideism

In matters pertaining to Divine Truth every Christian should be on his guard against two extremes: the extreme of an anti-intellectual fideism, on the one hand, and that of a certain type of rationalism, on the other. Fideism is an attitude of mind which tends to disparage reason. Rationalism, on the other hand, minimizes the need for faith. Both of these attitudes are wrong and they are harmful because they are wrong.

2. Religion and Life

Religion is not, as many have supposed, a merely human enterprise in which man calls God to his aid. It is a divine enterprise in which God calls man to His side.

3. The Use of Reason and the Goal of Life

What kind of insanity is it that can impel a man to make a completely patient, refined, and meticulous use of his reasoning powers in matters of secondary, even trivial import, when his basic attitude toward the goal of life itself is unsettled, whimsical, and left to the shifting opinions of amateurs?

4. The Nature of Man and the Meaning of Christian Life

The true meaning of a genuinely Christian life is unintelligible except with reference to its ultimate end or goal, man's union and happiness with God. Moreover, it is not through any kind of natural instinct that man tends toward his goal. Every agent seeks its goal in a manner proportioned to its nature, and it is the nature of man as an intelligent and voluntary agent to tend toward *his* goal through knowledge and love. On a purely natural basis the life of man as man is most fully achieved when all of his other activities, like the use of the senses and his emotional responses, are presided over by his intelligence and subjected to the well-ordered movement of his will. Yet beyond this, we must acknowledge that the life of Christian man — so far as knowledge is concerned — is preeminently a life of Faith. Our Faith is or should be the exemplary cause of all of our activities as Christians; it is the substance of things to be hoped for; the evidence of things to come.

*   *   *

The assent to the truths of Faith is for many Christians too facile, too nominal, too ephemeral to allow these truths to penetrate to the very bone and marrow of their lives. Somehow the knowledge of these truths does not terminate in the other theological virtues, those of hope and love.

*   *   *

We have been reminded by one of the great wise men of our times that just as a living faith must change the life of the believer, so a living religion must influence and transform the social way of life — the culture.

5. Dawson on Christianity and Secular Culture

"As there is an organic relation between the Christian faith and the Christian life, so also there is a relation between Christian life and Christian culture. The relation between faith and life is completely realized only in the life of the saint. But there has never been a temporal society of saints, and the attempt to create one, as in Puritan England or Massachusetts, represents a sectarian perversion of Christian culture. Nevertheless it is the very nature of the Christian Faith and the Christian life to penetrate and change the social environment in which they exist, and there is no aspect of human life which is closed to this leavening and transforming process." Christopher Dawson, *The Crisis of Western Education* (New York: Sheed & Ward, 1961), pp. 138–139.

* * *

"The Catholic scholar may decide to ignore the secular culture that surrounds him and concentrate his whole attention on the Christian culture of the past when the whole of life was governed by religious principles, and art and architecture and philosophy existed to serve the Church. By doing so, he creates a kind of Christian ghetto. . . ." *Ibid.*, p. 152.

* * *

"One must bring home to the average man that religion is not a pious fiction which has nothing to do with the facts of life, but that it is concerned with realities, that it is in fact the pathway to reality and the law of life. This is no easy task, since a completely secularized culture is a world of make-believe in which the figures of the cinema and the cartoon strip appear more real than the figures of the gospel." *Ibid.*, p. 175.

6. The Need for Christian Solidarity

One of the great needs of our times is the need for ecumenical unity — the need for a realization of the Petrine ideal of a single, united people, a *gens sancta* that can present a united front against all the forces of evil in the modern world. As Christopher Dawson points out, Christianity still exists as a living theological and spiritual tradition, but it has been gradually deprived of intellectual and social influence on modern culture. Yet it has something to offer of which modern technological society is in desperate need — namely, a principle of spiritual coordination and a principle of unity.

*   *   *

The facts of life as we know them, our daily work and play, our scientific discoveries and technological advancements, the growth of civilization, everything takes its ultimate truth and value from within the total context of an overall religious view of life.

VIRTUE AND THE CHRISTIAN LIFE

1. The Meaning of Love

As a Christian philosopher I am a bit wary of the axiom that virtue has its own reward. This motto is a bit too stoic to be ultimately convincing to anyone who knows that the reward of true virtue is not virtue itself but love. In the wise words of Jacques Maritain: "The perfection of human life is a perfection of the art of loving and not of the art of perfecting ourselves and of being sufficient unto ourselves in our intelligence, our strength, or our virtue." J. Maritain, "The Humanism of St. Thomas," from *Living Schools of Philosophy*, ed. by D. Runes (Ames, Iowa: Littlefield, Adams, and Co., 1956), p. 267.

* * *

Love seeks its union through activity, and it is the sort of activity by which the lover adjusts *himself* to the desires of his beloved. In this sense *love always involves a displacement*, a "putting of oneself out," a discomfort, that knowledge by itself does not. In knowing something we do not have to change our lives for that which we know; in loving something — we must. As St. Augustine would have it, Amor meus, pondus meum — "My love is my weight." "It is my love that weighs me down."

Further, love has a way of stirring us up to do things — to dance, to cook, to get dressed for dinner — things we might never do without love. All of this because the lover in a sense no longer has a life of his own, because he lives for the one whom he loves. In the words of St. Thomas: "A lover is placed outside of himself and made to pass into the object of his love, inasmuch as he wills good to the beloved and works for that good by his providence even as he works for his own" (*Summa Theologiae* I, Q. 20, a. 2, *ad lum*). To love someone, then, is nothing more than to will *and to do* what is good for the object of our love.

2. *Piety and Pietism*

There is a big difference between piety and pietism. *Piety* is the love and devotion that a true Christian bears toward his Father, God. It is a sense of loyalty, fidelity, love, and devotion all wrapped in one. It is a predisposition to do God's will wherever the path may lead and, being above all else something personal, its focal point lies outside the love of oneself. By contrast *pietism* is a certain type of religious formalism that turns its back on the realities of the secular order in which it exists. The religious pietist is one who, keeping his religion pretty close to his belt, has no keen sense either of a personal relationship with God or of the religious and social needs of his fellowman. Pietism is based on a spirit of withdrawal from the world — not in order to save it — but to save oneself lest one be contaminated by the evil it contains. Thus too it is most often associated with a certain type of jansenism and puritanism. The roots of pietism, however, are to be found in a certain type of spiritual pride and ambition that would make one's love of God a purely private affair.

3. *The Perfection of Christian Life*

"The greater a virtue is, the more it withdraws a man even from less grievous sins; just as the more perfect health is, the more does it ward off even minor ailments." *Summa Theologiae*, I-II, Q. 73, a. 5 c.

*   *   *

In the Christian view of man it is not ordinarily possible for man (as is the case with the angels) to achieve his perfection all at once. This means, of course, that everyone is given in his lifetime a certain margin of trial and error, or a "second chance." What is important, therefore, is that each person avail himself not only of the "second" chance, but of every new opportunity that comes his way to reform and improve his life. To speak here in the language of theology, a man cannot indefinitely and repeatedly refuse with impunity the grace that is offered him, for sooner or later he will have made his final choice.

4. Counsel and Prudence

It is false magnanimity to think that we can accomplish great deeds without proportionate means, and proportionate means includes the use of counsel as a part of prudence. Also, if the counsel goes against the grain, we should not reject it but rather have the humility to modify, postpone, or even abandon our plans as the situation may require. Much grief could be avoided by seeking counsel when needed from the right person and adhering strictly to that person's judgment about what is to be done or not to be done. *To take counsel is the mark of a prudent man.*

*   *   *

"Some men, insofar as they are good counsellors in matter of warfare, or seamanship, are said to be prudent officers or pilots, but not prudent absolutely; for only *those are prudent absolutely who give good counsel about what concerns man's entire life.*" Summa Theologiae, I–II, Q. 57, a. 4, ad 3um.

5. Simplicity

Simplicity is always preferable to multiplicity and complication. For example, it is far more perfect to accomplish an action in a relatively simple manner than by means of subterfuge, trial, and error. If a football player can make a touchdown at once and by means of a long run (rather than by all sorts of short plays), then so much the better. Or if a writer can equivalently express in a paragraph an idea that takes another writer two or three paragraphs to express, he is the better writer for that. Too, we regard as more perfect — not a simpleton — but a person who is endowed with a simplicity of good taste, good dress, good manners, and the like. In a word, simplicity is a Godlike perfection which only few persons possess to a high degree.

*   *   *

The simple person is one who does the most with the least element of fanfare and drama. He or she is the sort of person that can quickly size up the circumstances of a given situation and act with a minimum of deliberation; a person who has a sure instinct, not only for the right, but for the best course of action. Simplicity in this sense is closely allied to the simplicity of the saints. It does not in any way imply stupidity, simplemindedness, or naïveté. What it does imply is a straightforwardness and a singleness of purpose, the absence of insincerity, of hypocrisy, of deceit, of "double-dealing," of lying, and of simulation. It is the one virtue that is most needed in modern life because it is most directly calculated to heal the split within the consciousness of man, between the force of his perverse habits and his desire to do the good. Once this virtue is acquired it will give a person a certain steady realism of outlook, a certain straightforwardness that will unflinchingly lead one to his goal.

*   *   *

6. Wisdom

Wisdom is no ordinary product of a routine educational process, nor does it achieve its full effect until it becomes an all-encompassing feature of our lives, until every facet of our lives is dominated from above by the light of this great virtue. True wisdom is achieved only when we break through the *sound barriers of words* to pierce their inner meaning, when we begin to learn the language of silent thought and the peace of deep understanding.

MAN AND SOCIETY:
DEMOCRACY AND AMERICAN LIFE

1. Why We Should Study the Greeks

To learn something about our present situation we are often told to go back to the Greeks, and this is not a bad bit of advice. The reason, however, for studying Greek art, literature, and philosophy is never to dig up the relics of the past for the mere sake of knowing the past. For one thing we study the Greeks to get to know something of the origin of Western civilization as we know it today. Or again, if we are Christians, we study the Greeks to know how their ideas influenced the subsequent development of Christian philosophy, theology, and art. A third reason is nonhistorical: we study the Greeks to learn from them whatever universal element of truth they provide in their approach to man and human institutions. It is for this last reason that the study of the Greeks has permanent significance for the whole of mankind.

2. Marxism

The dialectical materialism of Karl Marx represents a one-sided view of man which fails to regard the higher and spiritual dimension of his being. It is a system of collectivism which reduced the individual human person to part of a larger whole — a nameless class. The appeal that this philosophy has is based on an insistent recognition of the urgency of man's economic needs. Such insistence is, of course, both legitimate and indispensable; yet the deficiency of Marxism as a philosophy of life is its failure to account for the reality of man's cultural, moral, and, above all, his authentically religious needs.

3. Naturalism in America

In contrast to Marxism, secularistic naturalism, such as we find it on the American continent, has placed a solid measure of emphasis on the dignity of the human person, the rights of the individual, and the inviolability of human freedom. Philosophically speaking, however, it is defective on two main counts: (1) its failure to explain the source of human freedom and intelligence and (2) its failure to direct human freedom to a goal that will satisfy the deepest aspirations that lie in the heart of man.

4. Democracy and Morality

Many persons find a great source of comfort and reassurance in "being on the side of democracy" which for them is "to be on the side" of right, truth, and goodness. Such persons fail to consider two important points: (1) that the ultimate source of responsibility, especially in a democracy, rests with the individual himself, and not on some vague collective whole; (2) that a democratic society (as well as any other) can for a lack of morality be corrupted from within and begin to degenerate even as have some of the worst forms of tyranny. In short, there is nothing in a democratic system that guarantees immunity from outside attacks or against corruption from within. As one of the early American orators has said: eternal vigilance is the price of liberty. We might also add that it is also the price of a sound system of morality.

5. Freedom and Finality: Abundance and Human Needs

The American economy is by and large an economy of abundance, and to some extent even an economy of surfeit as well. In such an economy the conscience of every individual should be primed to a realization of the needs of others. Failing this, there tends to be a forgetfulness both of spiritual and moral foundations of our national life, and to that extent a weakening of the foundations themselves.

*   *   *

In recent years Americans have overcompensated for their basic temporal needs, and only now are beginning to wonder what freedom in its larger sense is for. Granting, then, that America is in large measure a nation well fed, well clothed, and comfortably situated in modern suburban homes, the questions for Americans to ask are these: What are we doing to make the enjoyment of freedom meaningful, not only for ourselves, our families, our fellow citizens, but also and especially for those who are deprived of the most basic sorts of freedom in many other parts of the world? Consciously or otherwise, our search for national purpose is nothing more than a search to make the possession of freedom a meaningful event in our human lives. It is the search to interpret the meaning of freedom in other than purely negative terms, such as the freedom from want, from fear, from oppression, from tyranny, and the like.

6. Morals and Legislation

Enlightened self-interest compels us to reexamine the level of morality in our society. And suppose that philosophers, moralists, and theologians consciously address themselves to this task. In such an event, every citizen, or at least those that are somewhat enlightened, should predispose himself as a citizen, not merely for self-applause in regard to areas of moral strength, but self-criticism where there is moral decadence or decay. Nor should anyone suppose that bad morals can be corrected by good legislation, as though one could legislate morality. There is a sense, however, in which good legislation is conducive to morality, and here the government should play an active role, that is, by making adequate provisions for public housing, conservation, recreation, and the like, and by insuring that no one is deprived of the benefits of such legislation because of his race, national background, or religion.

7. Reflections on America: Jacques Maritain

". . . Among the general features of American psychology, and despite many exceptions, of course, I think we can observe a certain proneness to a peculiar sort of impatience, and, as a result, a proneness also to quick discouragement . . .(Although) American crowds (when waiting for a train, for instance) are incomparably more patient than French crowds . . . they are not patient with life . . . They get disturbed and discouraged very soon, if the work they have undertaken is slow to succeed." Jacques Maritain, *Reflections on America* (New York: Charles Scribners Sons, 1958), p. 44.

* * *

"There is an American *modesty* before life and reality which is a great moral virtue and a dynamic quality of considerable efficacy. It originates, I think, in a sense of the complexity of things; of the fluidity of life which escapes our concepts; and of the multiple aspects of reality which make our judgments precarious." *Ibid.*, p. 96.

* * *

"This country should never, and will never, give up the experimental approach, which is a blessing for it; but it would be quite beneficial for it to develop, at the same time, an adequate ideological formulation, an explicit philosophy, expressing its own ideal in communicable terms. This does not mean, of course, that it would be advisable to manufacture an ideology for the sake of propaganda, God forbid! It means that the development of a greater general interest in ideas and universal verities is a presupposed condition without which no genuine possibilities of intellectual communication can emerge." *Ibid.*, p. 118.

*   *   *

"It would seem that this country fosters belief in the goodness of Nature, the natural goodness of Man in the Rousseauist sense. Everything would be all right if Nature were not repressed, and were left to its own inclinations. In other words, there is no hidden root of evil in our nature, no original sin, no need for divine grace. In this way of thinking . . . we have to do with a trend toward naturalism more insidious, I think, than the threat of materialism. . . . Yet there is some serious inconsistency in this very naturalism, because we are confronted with a quite opposite tendency, originating, I think, in a residue of (and bitterness against) old Puritanism. And from this other point of view Nature is not so good. There is an idea that human nature is fundamentally miserable — a set of brute instincts and desires which clash with each other, and which are not disciplined from within by moral conscience, to be sure, but only repressed from without by social taboos." *Ibid.*, pp. 131–132.

8. American Activism

The American tradition is not, by and large, one of leisure, but of work. Most Americans, whatever their philosophical persuasion or religious belief, feel at least some sense of historical continuity with the Puritan heritage of the past. This heritage is one of a rigorous commitment to a life in which the order of the day is (whether for religious or secular motives) to *get things done*. On the other hand, some economists are beginning to predict that the American society of the future — thanks to automation — will largely be a "workless" society — a society of consumers, not producers. If this prediction is only in some measure true, there will be the need for some radical readjustments in the "American way of life," not the least of which is the knowledge of how to make the best use of one's leisure time.

9. World Peace

The problem of achieving world peace is more than a technical problem of diplomatic and military strategy. Contrary to a somewhat misleading popular slogan we don't simply "wage peace" — but we try to establish an orderly set of conditions that will naturally lead to peace.

10. Repression and the Good Society

Only dissatisfaction and discontent result if men are rendered inactive and useless. Under such conditions the only natural human response is one of revolt. Such a revolt, moreover, if it spills over into overt action, can be contained only by a corresponding measure of repression from without, and repression of this sort is always an affront to the dignity of the human person, an insult to his human intelligence and freedom. *A good society, then, not only declares that the individual is free, it strives to promote those conditions that make it possible for every citizen to exercise his freedom in a way that is meaningful to the overall end of life.*

11. Man an Historical Animal

Man is an historical animal: not only does he have a tradition, he is *conscious* of having it, and naturally tends to preserve that tradition if it is in any way suited to his nature. As Josiah Royce once remarked, *man is a being who lives with his past.*

12. Need for a New Christian Culture in America

The American consciousness is in a sense a "split consciousness." This split is between an unrealistic type of idealism (whose roots are traceable all the way back to the spiritualistic transcendentalism of Jonathan Edwards) and a shallow type of realism. The problem that Christians face today in America is the problem of healing this split within our culture. The solution can come about only by working toward a new philosophy and a new culture which, though idealistic, never degenerates into a stoical or puritanical view of man's nature, and which, though realistic, never becomes purely pragmatic. In short, the problem is to work out — to recapture, if necessary — an integral type of philosophy that will give some guarantee of the real basis of human freedom and true social solidarity.

CHRISTIAN CHALLENGES AND IDEALS

1. Challenges to Modern Christianity

Today's challenge as it faces the modern Christian is that of restoring a true Christian culture as the antidote to the vague and offbeat stirrings within our society. It is the challenge of reasserting the spiritual nature of man and of human freedom.

* * *

The energies of Christians will forever remain latent and therefore be spoiled unless those who believe in Christ respond to the challenges of their times. Every Christian should, of course, depend upon divine grace to meet these challenges but if he depends on divine grace without some outlay of effort on his part, he is being presumptuous. The triumph of God's grace and providence is in a sense inevitable but only in the sense of presupposing that Christians bend their best human efforts toward achieving their goals.

2. Mediocrity

The problem with many Christians today is not a lack of morality or a sense of dedication to the faith. Theirs is the problem rather of taking these things for granted, and in so doing of becoming like the foolish virgins of the Gospel, chaste, but not especially distinguished for the use of their intelligence in those things that are of the highest concern, such as one's total Christian involvement in the world of politics, law, and business.

3. Building Up a New Christian Culture

Every Christian should know something of the Church if only to know the tradition of scholars and saints to which he belongs and with a view toward making that tradition relevant to the ferment of his times. Let us make no mistake about it: Christian civilization is much larger and richer than the wisdom of any one man or culture. It is much more expansive than our own American version of it, which is in too many respects tainted with the corroding deposits of jansenism, puritanism, and pragmatism. It is the expanse and grandeur of Christian civilization that every Christian must somehow be made either to discover or rediscover for himself.

4. Ideas and Social Action

Whenever we wish to act intelligently our conduct must be guided by *ideas*. It is our ideas which serve, in other words, as the exemplars or patterns of all the activity we perform. Even so, one should also remember that ideas of themselves don't do anything. In the language of philosophy what is needed to get things done is an "efficient cause."

5. Need for Social Justice

One of the scandals to the mind of unbelievers is the rampant unconcern on the part of many believers for social justice. Here we might well apply the too little known dictum of the great William James: "The sentimentalist fallacy is to shed tears over abstract justice and generosity, beauty, etc., and never to know these qualities when you meet them in the street *because the circumstances make them vulgar*."

6. Christian Cosmism and Christian Humanism

One of the great challenges of our times is to develop a

new type of Christian "cosmism" and humanism that fully harmonize with all the advances of modern science and modern psychology. It is no mere accident that St. Paul himself took a cosmic view of the world, placing emphasis on the sense of solidarity that should exist, on the one hand, between man and his fellowman, and, on the other, between man and the rest of nature. In contrast to all forms of naturalism, Christian cosmism is never to be taken as a view of the cosmos without God, but one that sees the universe for all the excitement which only a divine plan could pack into it. No Christian should ever allow himself to forget that the natural goods of the world in which we live are *real* goods: they add pleasure and give dignity to human life, they give it a new dimension. Viewed, then, in its fuller light Christian cosmism blossoms forth into a true Christian humanism. Such a humanism is based on an unqualified recognition of the intrinsic worth of every human being as existing *sui juris* and never for the sake of a utilitarian end — good or bad.

7. Optimism and Pessimism

Between the faulty optimism of certain pragmatists (which is based on an ignorance of original sin) and the radical pessimism of certain existentialists like Sartre, there is a Christian point of view which regards the universe and man with it as the handiwork of God but also sees particular dangers in one's becoming too much attached to the world for its own sake. This does not involve a denial of the intrinsic worth of human values, such as the value of art — but it does point up the need for subordinating them to a divine plan.

8. Wisdom and Its Restoration

As a Christian philosopher I have but one vested concern which is the restoration of wisdom on all levels within our society. What I have in mind is not a particular wisdom or prudence in the sense that it is restricted in scope to a single category of human experience. There is such a thing as the wisdom of the politician with respect to winning an election, of the businessman with respect to sales and profits, of the doctor with respect to the comfort and cure of his patients, etc. Such wisdoms, however, acquire their ultimate significance from their subordination to the total good of man as regards his final end.

9. Knowledge and Love

There is nothing incompatible between knowledge and love, for true knowledge, when it blossoms forth into wisdom, implies not only the possession of truth but the love of the Good. The wise man, therefore, is he who in the Christian scheme of things is committed with the totality of his being to the goods both of nature and grace. He understands in order to love, and he loves in order to understand. The wise man is humble in the presence of mystery; patient in time of doubt. He is quick to forget the irrelevant; careful to remember what is sound. It is he who has the courage to conquer himself and the incomparable grace of knowing how to love his neighbor whatever the circumstances may be. By an instinct of nature and of grace he knows when to be silent, when to speak, and his view is likened to God's view of things — for he regards temporal events from the perspective of a goal that lies outside of time.

FIRST THINGS AND LAST

1. Rule of Life

Like any kind of rule or measure a "rule of life" is meant to establish order and control. It determines in advance how one should act if a given set of circumstances arise. It is like a "principle" as when we say that so-and-so is a "man of principle" or a "man of his word" and not the victim of his own whims and impulses. It is a plan or a program that one adheres to in spite of contrary winds. It is a pattern, a model, an "exemplary cause," that directs the course of our lives.

2. On Being Alive

In the view of St. Thomas a thing is said to live insofar as it operates of itself and not insofar as it is moved by another. If, therefore, a person is "alive," he won't have to wait to be pushed but will act — with God's help — on his own.

3. Decision-Making

The making of decisions is less a matter of the intellect than it is of the will. Most often what we mean when we say that we cannot make up our *minds* is that we cannot make up our *wills*, and failing this we resort to the lazy man's technique of "stalling for time."

4. Conversion

The medievals, St. Bonaventure in particular, often used a beautiful Latin phrase to signify man's need for looking up to God. They spoke of it as a *conversio mentis ad Deum* ("the turning of the mind to God"). By the word "mind," however, they did not simply mean reason or intellect *as a thing apart*, but *all* of the powers of soul . . . our senses, our feelings, our subconscious, our intellect, our will, our entire being. Man's whole "ontological posture" should be directed toward God.

5. Humility and Obedience

Whenever God speaks through His prophets, His saints, or through His Church, it is not the role of man to question, to criticize, or to deny — but to accept with joy the message of salvation that has been offered him and to put that message to work in his day-to-day life.

*   *   *

Humility before being should mean above all a desire on the part of man to acquiesce in his radical contingency, and in so doing to acknowledge his complete and utter dependence upon God as his Creator, his Redeemer, and the Universal Provider of all of his needs.

*   *   *

Obedience means in practice submitting to the plan of life that God has for you. How do you know this plan? Not by reading God's mind, but by your own mature and responsible judgment as to what is best for you in the concrete circumstances of your life.

6. "Fast Living"

Nothing is more obvious to man — and in a sense more painful — than the limitations he suffers with respect to time. As Heidegger puts it, *man is a being who knows that he is going to die.* His entire life as it were is overshadowed by the consciousness of his death. With this thought in mind many persons try to "cheat" time by "living it up," that is, by accelerating the movement of their lives, but *not* toward the goal intended for them. To become *real* cheaters they must learn how to beat time all of the way, that is, by latching on to eternity. Thanks to revealed truth man can know through faith that he has the promise of eternal life — a share in the very eternity of God Himself, and herein lies his only salvation. Although man, therefore, knows that he is going to die, he knows much more: that beyond death there is for him the promise of eternal life.

7. Death

Modern paganism will not allow us to look death in the face or to think that death is inevitable. Well, the fact of the matter is that death *is* inevitable. Even so, it is *not* inevitable that we take a fatalistic view of death, for the *kind* of death we face, or at least our manner of facing it, will depend in large measure on the kind of life we have led. A happy life can only provide the way for a happy death as well.

8. Loneliness

We should never allow ourselves to be lonely except in the practical sense that it is ultimately we who with God's help must make certain decisions on our own. Never, however, should we be lonely in the sense of brooding over our situation as though no one were present to share it. In the Christian view this kind of loneliness is incompatible with the providence of God. Unhappily, it is *this* kind of loneliness that plagues the heart of modern man — a loneliness that paves the way to despair. The remedy, then, is a good solid dose of Christian hope and joy, a complete abandonment of oneself — recklessly — to God's care, not our own.

TECHNOLOGY AND THE HUMAN CONDITION

1. Technology and the Decline of Wisdom

Never before has man accumulated such a vast storehouse of knowledge for himself. Yet the rise of knowledge in the form of science and technology has marked, paradoxically a decline of the order of wisdom. While it is true, therefore, that man knows how to project himself into outer space (no small accomplishment!), he has also forgotten how to live. The contrast that exists, then, is typified by man's knowledge of the world, on the one hand, and his ignorance, partial or total, of his original nature and end.

2. Scientism and the Problem of Human Existence

Many persons hold forth the promise of solving on scientific and technological grounds what they regard as the "riddle" of human existence. In their view man is purely and simply a biological product of the evolutionary forces in nature; he is an immanent product of nature. More than this, it is claimed that through human intelligence alone — itself an outgrowth of nature — man will provide for himself and independently of revelation the solution to all of his problems, the answer to all his needs. Such persons deny that man has any transcendent goal *beyond the physical universe* and assert that man's whole life is the fulfillment of his temporal aims. This attitude — most appropriately designated as scientism — is based on the complete denial of the real mystery of human existence.

3. The Limits of Technology

Leave it to sociologists and social psychologists to describe in more ample terms how the inventions of modern life have radically affected not only the external aspects of modern living but also man's very outlook on reality itself. This point should be stressed, however: man no longer feels himself in close contact with nature nor in deep social communion with his fellowman. His roots, in other words, are no longer in the soil, and in the absence of his former sense of social solidarity (together with all the cultural and religious traditions that it embodied) contemporary man has suffered a radical sense of insecurity, displacement, and loss. He is in a position of having little or no sense of continuity with the past, a feeling of deep discontentment with the present, and worst of all, anguish and insecurity as to the fulfillment of his future needs. Little wonder that the immersion of contemporary man in the products of the technology he has created has led to a profound sense of unhappiness and dread . . . and yet none of this need be so, provided that man use technology as his tool or instrument for human needs, and not the other way around.

*   *   *

Many persons in spite of their ignorance about the "end" of man are profoundly aware of the need for something in life that transcends technology. If this were not so, it would be impossible to explain the emergence of naturalistic sects, beatnik movements, centers of cultural pursuit, mystical fads, and the like. Even the rich man of our times is aware — if only in a visceral sense — that high-powered boats, luxury hotels, extended vacations in exotic climates cannot provide

*him with the ultimate satisfaction of what in point of fact,
if not in point of recognition, are his ultimate spiritual needs.*

*   *   *

Technology is here to stay. But will man continue to allow
his total outlook to be dominated by the hopes and fears of
technology or will he take these hopes and fears as mere
symptoms of the deeper spiritual longings of his nature?
Whether he admits it to himself or not, man is always in
quest of the Infinite Good.

*   *   *

A truly Christian outlook does not look with disdain on
technology. On the other hand, neither does it worship it as
an end in itself.

*   *   *

However much contemporary man may bury or lose himself in technology he cannot find his salvation there. Further,
if salvation does exist for man (and in the Christian view
there has never been any doubt on this score), it is pretty
important for each person to discover for himself where the
path of salvation lies.

*   *   *

It is easily possible for man to overrate the degree of satisfaction that technological control can provide in the overall
purpose of human life.

*   *   *

Two of the most difficult tasks of technology are to reduce
the barriers of space and the barriers of time. *The most
difficult task of all, however, is to break the barriers of human
communication itself, and this is something that cannot be
accomplished by technology alone.*

4. *Christianity and the New Culture*

The contemporary reaction to the preponderance of technology (wherever this reaction exists) is beginning to assert

itself in vague outlines as a new humanism. *It is a matter of crucial importance at such a critical moment in contemporary history that Christianity not only show itself capable of measuring up to this challenge but that it prove itself to be the very base of the new culture toward which we are emerging* — which is at once one of science, art, literature, philosophy, theology, all wrapped in one.

THE DIGNITY OF MAN AND HIS FREEDOM

1. Man Is His Own Master

To understand the real value of freedom reflect for a moment on the dismal but nonetheless real prospect of a completely regimented society, of a society that is the handiwork of "social engineers" who in their self-appointed role regard themselves, both theoretically and practically, as the wise men of the new technological era.

*   *   *

A truly democratic society is based on a profound recognition of the dignity of man and his freedom. While such a society, like any other, requires social planning, it should never make man the instrument of social engineers who arbitrarily determine for themselves the goals of human life. The traditional wisdom holds firm in its commitment to the doctrine that *there are certain built-in goals that are incurably a part of human nature itself.*

2. Dignity and Self-Assurance

Prerequisite to every moral and spiritual reform is a profound conviction of one's own dignity as a man. This means that it is impossible for a man to rise to a high-level challenge until he is convinced in his own mind that he is not only

capable, but *worthy* of the task. Thus every man must
strengthen himself, build up his confidence, be convinced
that he as a human being is of more worth than anything
else in the universe. It is for this reason (if no other) that
modern man must again rediscover for himself what a high-
level vocation it is to bear the dignity of a man.

*   *   *

Not only has modern man lost his vision of the reality of
God, but of his own basic nature as well. What is necessary,
therefore, is the double recovery both of himself, of his own
nature, and of the knowledge and love of God.

3. Freedom, Pride, and Grace

No doubt the most potent indication of the triumph of
human pride is the exaggerated emphasis on freedom. Man
today cherishes his freedom as if it were a god, and in so
doing tries to make himself like unto God.

*   *   *

Freedom for Dewey is the freedom for man to pursue
whichever goods he sees fit. While such a view is based in
a measure on fact, pressed too far it leads us back to the
relativism of the ancient Greek sophist, Protagoras, for whom
man is the measure of all things. Such a doctrine overlooks
the fact that man is *not* the measure of all things if only for
the reason that there are certain built-in tendencies ante-
cedent to human choice that impel man to choose what is
good in itself.

4. Heidegger on Responsibility and Freedom

"The only kind of personal identity which is open to us
(is) that of engaging ourselves in a final project up to the
very end by taking over the whole of our past just as we have
been, with all our imperfection and guilt, through a decisive
choice in the present moment." John Wild, "An English
Version of Martin Heidegger's 'Being and Time,'" *The Re-*

view of Metaphysics, Vol. XVI, No. 2 (Dec., 1962), p. 307.

*   *   *

"Heidegger shows how self-unity and wholeness must be achieved, if they are to be achieved at all, by resolute choice and action which take over the whole of a deficient past, and engage the whole of the future, seen only in the light of death, up to the very end." *Ibid.,* p. 309.

5. *The Surrender of Freedom*

If a man surrenders his freedom he surrenders all. The fear, then, of losing one's freedom is a well-grounded fear — for if one surrenders his freedom to the wrong persons, the wrong causes, the wrong things, in effect he surrenders *himself.*

6. *The Life of Man: Intelligence and Freedom*

The life of man is more perfect than anything else in nature, for man has the power to propose to himself the very end of the operations that he performs. True enough, the lower animals have knowledge, but it is knowledge of the sort that is limited to sensible things as such; moreover, it is the sort of knowledge that is exclusively related to their biological needs. Further, a brute has no way either of knowing what it does or why it engages in the operations it performs. Lacking a knowledge of the end of its operations, it is lacking also in that freedom by which it can direct itself to the end. By contrast, man as man has intelligence, and it is *through his intelligence that he can perceive both the end of his activities and the proportion of the means to the end.* In a word, the life of man as man is characterized by intelligence and freedom.

THE PURSUIT OF HAPPINESS

1. Philosophy and Happiness

The purpose of philosophy is not to confuse, but to clarify, and where perfect clarity is not to be had (as seldom it is) the philosopher at least should point the way in which the *truths of things* lie. Not the least of these truths is the truth of overriding importance for man as to the ultimate source of his happiness. Man more than anything else wants to know where his happiness lies and how to find it, and *if the philosopher himself is mute on this vital question, one may with very good reason hold suspect any claim that he makes to any superior wisdom.*

2. Happiness as a Gift of God

True happiness is a gift of a loving God. It is a grace which man implicitly longs for when he lacks it, and upon which he thoroughly depends even after he has received it. Without this grace, however, there can only be natural happiness and natural joy of the inadequate sort that terminates in finite goods. Thus the "hunger for the Infinite" can never be satisfied by the movement of the natural appetite alone, however intense that pursuit. Perhaps no one better than Augustine has expressed the fundamental need for the gift of charity when he said, *Noverim me — Noverim te —* "May I know myself, may I know Thee." Perhaps, too, no one more than Augustine realized to its fullest extent that the desire for God can be efficaciously fulfilled only by God Himself.

3. Happiness and Modern Man

"If modern man pretends to disdain happiness, he often does so because he has rendered himself incapable of it in the first place. By selling himself short, he comes to think that it would be impossible for him, and loses even the appetite for it. And that is the bottom of the abyss. If we would save men, the first thing we must do is *restore* at least their desire for salvation and their *confidence* that it is something possible for them." Jean Danielou, *The Scandal of Truth*, trans. by W. J. Kerrigan (Baltimore: Helicon Press, 1962), p. 45.

* * *

"The hide-and-go-seek between happiness and man is a strange game indeed. Happiness hides itself from those who pursue it, and tags the players who are not looking for it. Like the Spirit, it breathes where it will. . . . Admittedly, one sure way never to be disappointed is never to expect anything. Yet that wisdom, too, falls short. For happiness is man's vocation. It is better to suffer and not renounce happiness than to find peace by renouncing it. *The man of courage is the man who continues to believe in happiness despite all failures and all disappointments.* And, in the end, happiness will never fail to show such a man its true face." *Ibid.*, pp. 45–46.

* * *

Happiness lies in the fulfillment of our fundamental needs, not our superfluous ones. Hence the reason why modern culture has produced a sense of unhappiness in contemporary man is that it has distracted him from his fundamental needs, such as his need for God, and made the superfluous ones seem necessary.

* * *

Man's greatest fear is that happiness may never be attainable for him, and it is in the depths of such anxiety — when no satisfactory solution is forthcoming — that man frequently gives himself up to despair. What anyone in such a position overlooks is that a universal remedy has been provided for all of mankind and this remedy is to be found in the redemptive grace of the God-Man Himself.

WORK, CONTEMPLATION, AND ACTION

1. The Need for Balance

Anxiety caused by useless tensions, imaginary problems, and the like produces the baneful effect of a loss of personal unity. I do not mean here the ontological unity of body and soul which is lost only by separation at death, but the unity that exists between a person's desires and the ultimate end of his nature as a man. To be at one with oneself a person must above all conform to his own true nature. Above all else each person should secure a balance in his life between action and contemplation.

2. The Pythagoreans

The old Pythagoreans regarded their philosophy as a way of life and they compared life itself to a game at the Olympics where three classes of persons were present: the venders, the athletes, and the spectators. In their view the venders played the "meanest" role of all because they came to the games only for commercial gain; the athletes played a yet higher role, which was to play in the games. The best role, however, was reserved for the spectators who came for the enjoyment of the game.

3. Man a Contemplative Animal

As a Christian philosopher I have never tired of repeating that man as much as anything else is a contemplative animal.

If modern experience has obscured this fundamental truth, the reason is not that the nature of man has radically changed, but that the cult of noise and distraction has taken the place of silence in our lives. Contemplation is above all else a hidden wisdom, a method of silent pursuit.

4. *The Christian Intellectual and His Work*

Religious zeal is never a substitute for learning, nor is there an intrinsic connection between being a scholar and being a saint. There are many saints who, even if they choose to become scholars, would be poor ones indeed. Yet given the vocation of a Christian intellectual, there is no stronger motive for becoming a scholar than that of becoming a saint. For the Christian intellectual who is intent on becoming a saint is one who knows that the fulfillment of his vocation lies *in* and *through* his work. Such a person knows, moreover, that the order of grace never destroys, nullifies, or derogates from the development of his natural powers. On the contrary, grace is a principle that transforms and elevates the natural powers to a level of performance they could never achieve on their own.

5. *Thoughts from a Quaker Theologian*

"Any Christian philosophy of work must search out the man behind the workman. It is bound to lay bare the fact that the man who shuffles through his prayers, if he says any . . . who paces the street at night to resolve a moral dilemma, is the same man who at work stands at the lathe or the punch press. . . . And it is my thesis that the contemplative element in terms of a frame of meaning . . . is a decisive factor in what happens to man in his work." Douglas V. Steere, *Work and Contemplation* (New York: Harpers and Brothers, 1957), p. ix.

*   *   *

"There is a contemplative hunger in each man, no matter

how deeply it is buried, that craves meaning, worth, 'importance' in his work. . . . A man yearns for some outlet, even if it be on the most simple scale, for his own potential levels of skill and ingenuity. *He longs to be able to feel that the product of his work is honestly valuable and needed.*" *Ibid.*, pp. 1–2.

*   *   *

"The frills of a society may be dazzling, its so-called production may be phenomenal, its material standard of living may be luxurious, but unless in its work men find a sense of their validity, and a place where they can grow and spend themselves, the vindicating factor is missing, and that society is doomed. . . ." *Ibid.*, p. 5.

*   *   *

"Human work is the intentional focusing of sufficiently disciplined and directed energy upon the dream, or the design, or the musical score, *to effect its realization in some tangible medium.*" *Ibid.*, p. 85.

*   *   *

"Unless out of [his] work some reason, some satisfying meaning, appears, work as such is not good for man. On the contrary work may be destructive." *Ibid.*, p. 20.

*   *   *

"It is because man is a contemplative being that he cannot bear a condition of meaninglessness, of irresponsibility, without its rotting him out." *Ibid.*, p. 21.

*   *   *

"Tolstoy goes so far to insist that our own outraged nature will sooner or later revenge itself upon those who live only by the mind, or in paper work, or in trade, and who never encounter nature's resistances by the work of their bodies. Not only will their bodies grow soft and flat and flabby, but the very quality of their thought and their sanity itself will be undermined. . . . Schweitzer, like Tolstoy, was convinced that the mind of man was not meant to be imprisoned in a sedentary animal. It requires a certain manual expression to keep its balance. Robbed of its manual expression, the mind goes askew and we get the shallow, rootless quality of thought that has so largely marked our time." *Ibid.,* pp. 91–93.

6. The "Little" Things

The life of the Christian should be one — ideally and really — of close and intimate union with God. This does not mean — far from it — that a devout Christian should be spending the better part of his day on his knees. Formal prayer is, of course, part of a Christian life, but the better part of one's day is engaged in details of ordinary life, and it is in the fulfillment of these details that one finds his happiness and peace.

7. A Word of Advice

Go about your work calmly, with all the sureness of a skilled workman who is quietly committed to the task at hand, following the method of "quiet pursuit." Find the joys of contemplation in your work and know that your work is a prayer. When you work it is yourself you offer to God. In the early morning get as close to nature as you can, gather up the sweetness of the morning dew, store up a few simple thoughts for the day. Don't be disturbed by anything — give the day to God. Don't become complicated: let your soul dilate in a simple contemplative gaze. Complete docility, attention to details, obedience to God's plan: herein lies the essence of the true Christian life. See the good in all things.

8. Need for a Christian Humanism

The growth of Christianity depends thoroughly on the responsible use of intelligence and freedom on the part of all of its members. What is important to know, therefore, is that the spirit of faith in no way demands the suppression of one's God-given faculty of intelligence, far less of the very sense themselves. What it does demand is an active and fruitful use of these powers so that the world of intellectuals, artists, and humanists, far from being repelled by the stupidity of believers, will be attracted by their perspicacity and intelligence.

SOME THOUGHTS ON CHRISTIAN EDUCATION

1. The Spirit of a True Education

A real education is not merely one that trains muscles, develops the mind, helps one to adjust socially and the like, but it is the sort of thing that enlarges and dilates the experience of the individual person beyond the limitation of all his previous environments. It is a process — or rather an adventure — that introduces the person into new and hitherto unsuspected worlds of artistic and speculative enjoyment. It is an experiment, if you will, that adds a new dimension to the life of the mind and one which directs itself toward helping each person discover his own creativity. A true education — in contrast to a purely mechanical one that only goes through the motions of learning — gives the individual a sense of his own personal dignity and worth and actually provides those conditions that make it possible for the student to participate more fully in the upward movement of the society in which he lives.

2. Dawson on Education and Life

"The Christian world of the past was exceptionally well provided with ways of access to spiritual realities. Christian culture was essentially a sacramental culture which embodied religious truth in visible and palpable forms: art and architecture, music and poetry and drama, philosophy and history, all were used as channels for the communication of religious truth. Today all these channels have been closed by unbelief or choked by ignorance, so that Christianity has been deprived of its means of outward expression and communication. It is the task of Christian education at the present time to recover these lost channels of communication and to restore contact between religion and modern society." Christopher Dawson, The Historic Reality of Christian Culture (New York: Harper & Brothers, 1960), p. 90.

*   *   *

"There exists a growing consciousness of the inadequacy of rationalism, alike as a philosophy of life and as a method of education. The influence of modern psychology above all has made men realize that their behavior is never entirely determined by rational motives. . . . Hence we are no longer satisfied with an education which confines the mind entirely to the sphere of rational consciousness, which cultivates the intelligence and starves the emotions, which ignores the existence of the unconscious forces in psychological life and concentrates its attention on the surface activity of the mind. For such an education inevitably produces an internal schism in personality and culture which is ultimately disastrous. Sooner or later the forces that have been ignored and repressed take their revenge and destroy the rational unity of the personality and the culture by their violent eruption into the sphere of consciousness." Ibid., p. 91.

*   *   *

"Human life . . . involves three different psychological levels. There is first the sub-rational life of unconscious instinct and impulse which plays such a large part in human life, especially the life of the masses. Secondly, there is the level of conscious voluntary effort and rational activity which is the sphere of culture, par excellence. And finally there is the super-rational level of spiritual experience, which is the sphere not only of religion but of the highest creative forces of cultural achievement — the intuitions of the artist, the poet, and the philosopher." *Ibid.*, p. 92.

*   *   *

"The great obstacle to the conversion of the modern world is the belief that religion has no intellectual significance; that it may be good for morals and satisfying to man's emotional needs, but that it corresponds to no objective reality. This is a pre-theological difficulty, for it is impossible to teach men even the simplest theological truths if they believe that the creeds and the catechism are nothing but words and the religious knowledge has no foundation in fact. On the other hand I do not believe that it is possible to clear the difficulty away by straight philosophical argument, since the general public is philosophically illiterate and modern philosophy is become an esoteric specialism. The only remedy is religious education in the widest sense of the word." *Ibid.*, pp. 89–90.

3. *Self-Transcendence*

What modern psychology has overlooked under the influence of Freud is the danger of the repression, not only of the emotional sources of human motivation and conduct, and, in general, the subrational, but above all the suprarational tendencies that are embedded in the nature of man. Man has an inherent need for transcending himself, a need for reaching up toward a goal that extends beyond the narrow boundaries of his own selfish goals, of his own ego, and it is the repression of this need for self-transcendence that can lead to even greater harm than the need for lower-level types of goods.

4. *Unfamiliarity With Mystical Tradition*

Very few Christians today, and among them Christian intellectuals, have a solid understanding of the mystical tradition of the Church. The tables of Mount Sinai are deeply engraved in the minds and hearts of many of our modern Christians, and if only by virtue of the laws of the Church they know something of the ascetical way. Yet when it comes to an understanding of the illuminative and unitive way, they are for all practical intents spiritual illiterates. Certainly there is no want of lip service to the great classical writers of the Christian mystical traditions. Yet these are the writers of whom it can be said: their names are indeed unforgotten (like St. Teresa and St. John of the Cross) but their works for the most part are unread.

*   *   *

As a Christian philosopher I would be the last to abandon the tradition of reason that has been fostered and encouraged by the Church. On the other hand, I reject the spirit of rationalism (wherever it exists) that closes the door to the mystical tradition both within and outside the Church. When philosophy as reason reigns supreme there is little room for what Nicholas of Cusa refers to as *intellectus*, as a mode of understanding that transcends a purely rational mode of discourse, and it is for reasons of this sort I presume that Nicholas of Cusa and others like Petrarch have written of their own ignorance and that of many other men. By contrast, if you want to know why existentialism is making such a powerful impact on the thinking of modern man the reason is that it gives some play to his mystical impulses, an opening to a kind of wisdom higher than reason can discover on its own. There were many reasons, indeed, why Bergson regards the mystics, the Catholic mystics in particular, as the supreme "geniuses" of the human race, and why Teilhard de Chardin has exalted what he calls mystical "science" as the highest of them all. Mind you I am not confusing philosophy with mysticism, but I am suggesting the need for an approach to philosophy that opens the door to the higher reaches of the mind and heart of man. Moreover, while I have touched on the subject I would suggest as a Christian philosopher that every program of Catholic learning should be deeply imbued with a consciousness of the mystical tradition of the Church. There is no reason why the existentialists alone should have a monopoly on the reality of the mystical approach.

5. The Liberal Dimension

"If we press too hard for more scientists — scientific quality will suffer or we will rob some other area of its creative people. We must have able men in government, able men in business, able men in the professions, our full share of creative output in literature and in the arts, no less than we need all of these things in science. *The society which creates scientists by diminishing the ranks of its philosophers may in the end have little need for either.*" A quotation from a speech delivered by Crawford H. Greenewalt, chairman of E. I. du Pont de Nemours and Company.

6. Problems and Mysteries: The Need for the Restoration of Intelligence

Not everyone is endowed with the habit of penetrating being as a mystery, as something which, though intelligible, can never be completely harnessed within the narrow confines of man's own vision of the world. Unfortunately, most persons have lost what Chesterton once called the "sense of mystery" and this because of a lack of a certain "humility before being." To them the all-important thing is to make things clear — *to subjugate the object*, to cut it down to the size of man's own limited intelligence. What cannot be made clear in the manner of Descartes or what cannot be verified in the manner of the logical empiricists does not for them exist. In the spirit of this approach to reality Dewey once said (perhaps with greater truth than he realized) that *a scientist without problems is an unhappy man.*

This problematic cast of mind is based on a rejection of the ability of the human intelligence to contemplate mysteries of any sort. The rejection of this function of intelligence has led on the natural plane to the consequent rejection of philosophy in its traditional sense as an unending pursuit of the natural mystery of being. On the supernatural level this rejection has led to the denial of the inherently objective worth of all religious doctrine and to the reduction of faith itself to what William James has called the will-to-believe. Faith is no longer knowledge (however obscure) of the living God, but a blind trust resulting in a subjective conviction of a nonexistent object!

Since contemporary man, then, has been robbed of the contemplative role of his human intelligence, he has been robbed of the natural mystery of being, including the mystery of his own being, and the supernatural mysteries of Faith. The restoration of the human intelligence will, by contrast, consist in showing that science does not have all the answers to life, and that the answers that philosophy and theology provide are equally as objective as those of science, though on a much higher plane.

7. Education and the Nature of Man

More than once Christopher Dawson has shown the great need through Christian education to restore the balance between the outer world of mechanized activity and the inner world of spiritual existence. This means in part that every person alive has a vested interest in coming to know through literature, art, history, and philosophy what his true nature is as a human person, and one of the great misfortunes of our times is that modern sophistry has obscured this vision man should have of himself. Myopia of this sort can be compensated for only by a realism in psychology that goes beyond the behavioristic approach to man, an approach that studies him from the limited biological point of view of biological stimulus and biological response. What everyone should know is that man is also a kind of being who is capable of a moral and spiritual stimuli and of moral and spiritual modes of response that altogether transcend his biological ones.

*   *   *

In the midst of an ever changing culture it is a question of prime importance and of the utmost urgency for men and women to rediscover themselves for what they are as human beings. Small consolation to the present generation that "man" will know more about himself in the future than he knows now, as though the "problem" of man will someday be completely solved. The point here is to recognize in the first place that man is never reducible to the level of a soluble problem, and second, that *the mystery of human existence must be newly reexamined* by each succeeding generation through whatever sources of knowledge are available, whether through psychology, philosophy, and, above all, through Revelation and theology.

*   *   *

A genuinely moral education should never enshackle life but help to fulfill it in terms of its most deep-rooted needs.

*   *   *

True education bases itself on the view that man is not just *homo rationalis*, a rational animal, but many things wrapped up in one: a worker (*homo faber*), a seeker of knowledge and wisdom (*homo sapiens*), a God-worshiping animal (*homo religiosus et mysticus*), an animal that likes to play sports (*homo ludens*), and finally an animal that likes to "poke fun at himself" (*homo risibilis*).

8. Use and Abuse

In every instance it is always necessary to distinguish between the use of a thing and its abuse. Thus the perversion of science is *scientism*; of history, *historicism*; of wisdom, *sophistry*; of education, *educationism*; of sense knowledge, *sensationalism*; and so on, and so on.

9. On the Teaching of Philosophy and Theology

No one will deny that the work of Christian education properly so called and conducted with the right motivation has in the language of theology a sacramental value as part of the "ministry of the word." On the other hand, it is sheer presumption to imagine or daydream that the work of education (whether it is Christian or not) can be carried on without (and I use here a favorite phrase of John Dewey's) the method of intelligence. On the part of Christian educators in particular it is sheer presumption to suppose that an unexamined approach to the teaching of such crucial subjects as philosophy and theology has a sort of sacramental effect ex opere operato. To the very contrary, I would say that philosophy and theology poorly taught — or taught according to some sort of brainwashing technique — not only has no sacramental effect, but can and sometimes does lead a young person away from the practice of his faith, which is to say, that it can often do more harm than good. I personally would rather see a young man go through college for four years without any philosophy at all than to have his mind totally prejudiced against it because he was badly taught or because it was forced down his throat after the manner of a bonum arduum. The point is, however, that this need not be so, and what is all-important is that Christian philosophers and theologians bend all of their efforts toward the presentation of the truths of their disciplines in a new and creative light.

*   *   *

It is the live intuitions of the professor of philosophy in the classroom that are calculated to produce more real and lasting convictions in the mind of the student than all the formal demonstrations in his textbook. Allow me, then, to interject Cardinal Newman's very relevant distinction between notional and real assent. A real assent is produced whenever a truth is presented as a "live hypothesis" that springs from the inner wellsprings of one's own personal convictions, and not merely as something that is worked out on paper, handed down, as it were, as a proposition to be respected or obeyed, but in no way personally assimilated. Truth becomes meaningful for a person only after one has made that truth his own, and there are few truths more profound in philosophy than the one which states that every act or perfection must be proportioned to the person who receives that act.

*   *   *

The Christian student, whether he attends a secular campus or not, needs philosophical formation as well as religious and spiritual formation. Both types of formation go hand in hand, and the one without the other can fall far short of the real intellectual and spiritual needs of the contemporary student. Moreover, as increasing numbers of Christian students attend the campuses of secular colleges and universities it is all the more important for their "elders" to provide them with a keen sense of direction. A "supermart" approach to philosophy a la the manner of Greenwich Village or a bohemian way of life can only lead to confusion. No undergraduate is as immature as most of his elders make him out to be or as mature as he makes himself to be.

INDEX